ONE

HUNDRED

GREAT

CATHOLIC

BOOKS

ONE HUNDRED GREAT CATHOLIC BOOKS

*From the Early Centuries
to the Present*

DON BROPHY

BlueBridge

Cover design by Per-Henrik Gurth

*Cover art by Art Resource, New York
(Michelangelo Buonarroti [1475–1564],
The Libyan Sibyl, Sistine Chapel)*

Text design by Jennifer Ann Daddio

Excerpts from the poetry of Jessica Powers are from
The Selected Poetry of Jessica Powers, published by ICS Publications, Washington, D.C.
All copyrights, Carmelite Monastery, Peewaukee, WI. Used with permission.

Excerpts from *The Poems of Gerard Manley Hopkins* (1970), edited by W. H. Gardner
and N. H. MacKenzie, are reprinted by permission of Oxford University Press.

Library of Congress Cataloging-in-Publication Data

Brophy, Donald, 1934-
One hundred great Catholic books :
from the early centuries to the present/Don Brophy.—1st ed.
p. cm.
Includes bibliographical references and index.
ISBN 1-933346-08-6
I. Catholic literature—Appreciation.   I. Title.
BX880.B76 2007
282—dc22
2007010195

Published by
BlueBridge
An imprint of
United Tribes Media Inc.
240 West 35th Street, Suite 500
New York, NY 10001

www.bluebridgebooks.com

Printed in the United States of America

1 3 5 7 9 10 8 6 4 2

CONTENTS

Introduction   *xiii*

The Desert Fathers: *Sayings and Stories*   *1*

Athanasius: *The Life of Antony*   *3*

Augustine of Hippo: *The Confessions*   *5*

John Cassian: *Conferences*   *7*

Benedict of Nursia: *The Rule of St. Benedict*   *9*

Anselm of Canterbury: *Prayers and Meditations*   *11*

Peter Abelard and Heloise: *The Letters*   *13*

Hildegard of Bingen: *Scivias*   *15*

Wolfram von Eschenbach: *Parzival*   *17*

Bonaventure: *The Soul's Journey into God*   *19*

Ugolino di Monte Santa Maria:
The Little Flowers of St. Francis of Assisi   *21*

Dante Alighieri: *The Divine Comedy*   *23*

Meister Eckhart: *Sermons*   *25*

Anonymous: *The Cloud of Unknowing*   *27*

Catherine of Siena: *The Dialogue*   *29*

Geoffrey Chaucer: *The Canterbury Tales*   *31*

Julian of Norwich: *Revelations of Divine Love*   33

Thomas à Kempis: *The Imitation of Christ*   35

Thomas More: *Utopia*   37

Ignatius Loyola: *Spiritual Exercises*   39

Bartolomé de Las Casas: *A Short Account of the
    Destruction of the Indies*   41

Teresa of Avila: *The Interior Castle*   43

Francis de Sales: *Introduction to the Devout Life*   45

John of the Cross: *The Dark Night*   47

Blaise Pascal: *Pensées*   49

Lawrence of the Resurrection: *The Practice of the Presence of God*   51

Jean-Pierre de Caussade: *Abandonment to Divine Providence*   53

John Henry Newman: *Apologia pro Vita Sua*   55

Pope Leo XIII: *Rerum Novarum*   57

Thérèse of Lisieux: *Story of a Soul*   59

Joseph Conrad: *Heart of Darkness*   61

G. K. Chesterton: *Orthodoxy*   63

Maria Montessori: *The Montessori Method*   65

Miguel de Unamuno: *The Tragic Sense of Life*   67

Gerard Manley Hopkins: *Poems*   69

Sigrid Undset: *Kristin Lavransdatter*   71

Karl Adam: *The Spirit of Catholicism*   73

John G. Neihardt: *Black Elk Speaks*   75

Étienne Gilson: *The Spirit of Medieval Philosophy*   77

François Mauriac: *Vipers' Tangle*   79

Georges Bernanos: *The Diary of a Country Priest*   81

Ignazio Silone: *Bread and Wine*   83

Caryll Houselander: *The Reed of God*   85

Evelyn Waugh: *Brideshead Revisited*   87

Thomas Merton: *The Seven Storey Mountain*   89

Christopher Dawson: *Religion and the Rise
of Western Culture*   91

Simone Weil: *Waiting for God*   93

Romano Guardini: *The End of the Modern World*   95

Ronald A. Knox: *Enthusiasm*   97

Graham Greene: *The End of the Affair*   99

Dorothy Day: *The Long Loneliness*   101

Pierre Teilhard de Chardin: *The Phenomenon of Man*   103

J. R. R. Tolkien: *The Lord of the Rings*   105

Flannery O'Connor: *A Good Man Is Hard to Find*   107

Alfred Delp: *Prison Writings*   109

Walter M. Miller, Jr.: *A Canticle for Leibowitz*   111

John Courtney Murray: *We Hold These Truths*   113

Walker Percy: *The Moviegoer*   115

Edwin O'Connor: *The Edge of Sadness*   117

J. F. Powers: *Morte D'Urban*   119

Pope John XXIII: *Journal of a Soul*   121

Vatican Council II: *The Documents*   123

Shusaku Endo: *Silence*   125

Xavier Rynne: *Vatican Council II*   127

Daniel Berrigan and Robert Coles: *The Geography of Faith*   129

William Johnston: *Christian Zen*   131

Henri Nouwen: *The Wounded Healer*   133

Avery Dulles: *Models of the Church*   135

Annie Dillard: *Pilgrim at Tinker Creek*   137

Paul Horgan: *Lamy of Santa Fe*   139

Bede Griffiths: *Return to the Center*   141

Andrew M. Greeley: *The Great Mysteries*   143

E. F. Schumacher: *A Guide for the Perplexed*   145

Anthony de Mello: *Sadhana*   147

Richard P. McBrien: *Catholicism*   149

Alasdair MacIntyre: *After Virtue*   151

John Main: *Word into Silence*   153

Ann Belford Ulanov and Barry Ulanov: *Primary Speech*   155

Gustavo Gutiérrez: *We Drink from Our Own Wells*   157

Hans Küng: *Why I Am Still a Christian*   159

Edith Stein: *Life in a Jewish Family*   161

Thomas Keating: *Open Mind, Open Heart*   163

Andre Dubus: *Selected Stories*   165

Jessica Powers: *Selected Poetry*   167

Ron Hansen: *Mariette in Ecstasy*   169

John P. Meier: *A Marginal Jew*   171

Elizabeth A. Johnson: *She Who Is*   173

Patricia Hampl: *Virgin Time*   175

Helen Prejean: *Dead Man Walking*   177

Pope John Paul II: *Crossing the Threshold of Hope*   179

Thomas Cahill: *How the Irish Saved Civilization*   181

James Carroll: *An American Requiem*   183

Raymond E. Brown: *An Introduction to the New Testament*   185

Robert Ellsberg: *All Saints*   187

Eamon Duffy: *Saints and Sinners*   189

Robert J. Schreiter: *The Ministry of Reconciliation*   191

Alice McDermott: *Charming Billy*   193

Ronald Rolheiser: *The Holy Longing*   195

Paul Lakeland: *The Liberation of the Laity*   197

Paul Elie: *The Life You Save May Be Your Own*   199

Afterword: And Fifty More   201

Book Notes   207

Index   217

Acknowledgments   222

TO PAT

for obvious reasons

INTRODUCTION

Books in the sense that we know them today are creatures of European-Christian culture. Of course writing existed for millennia before the Christian era, but in the beginning people wrote on scrolls, or on clay or wax tablets. These were awkward, not easily portable, and more suitable for public use than private reading. The development of parchment (prepared animal hides) in the early Christian era offered a new way to capture writing. Medieval monasteries employed scores of monks to copy manuscripts—easier done on a codex of separate sheets than on long scrolls. In this way pages evolved. At first these were simply stacked in piles; later they were sewn together. And so the book was born. Eventually, with the advent of paper in Europe and the invention of the printing press, the modern, mass-produced book came into being—many steps of the long process driven by the desire to spread the Christian message.

Then and now, believers have treasured books. Initially they were precious because they were few in number, but also because books held the wisdom of the ages. We still value them—those of us who have grown up reading. Books are our friends and our treasures. There are books on many of our shelves right now that we may never read again but which we keep because the initial experience of reading them was so memorable. Their physical presence speaks of past delights and lessons learned. They are doors opening on familiar rooms, voices calling from other places.

Probably each of us could create a list of books that have been significant in our lives. The list would likely include books of all sorts—textbooks, professional books, fiction, politics, history, art, humor, travel manuals, a user manual for the computer, nature books. Each list, each book, has its own memories.

Books from a religious or spiritual tradition have a special place in such a list. They do more than simply impart information: Like C. S. Lewis's wardrobe, they take us into another realm, into mystery. They are not merely words—they bring us closer to the original Word beyond language. The best and most memorable of them burn with an inner fire, burn without being consumed. Take off your shoes when you read them.

This volume names one hundred books that have nourished Catholic Christians and many other seekers over the centuries. There is no claim being made that these are the one hundred "best" books or the one hundred "most important" Catholic books. This is not a contest. They are not ranked in any way or compared to one another. They are simply one hundred books, chosen because they approach classic status (at least the older ones) and are considered worthy by readers to this day. But every choice is naturally subjective—the "greatness" of any book is a subjective matter. The brief summaries on these pages try to place them in historical context, give a short digest of their contents, and suggest what the experience of reading these books—some of them quite old—is like for a contemporary reader.

Of course calling a book "Catholic" is really a misnomer—people are Catholic, books are not. So in developing this list of titles it was decided at the outset to include primarily books whose authors are Catholic—meaning Roman Catholic, not Anglo-Catholic (without implying disrespect to the Anglicans). This, however, invites further objections. Were the Desert Fathers Roman Catholic? Was John Cassian? These individuals lived before the Roman and Orthodox churches began to split apart. Cassian is included here, but later Greek and Russian Orthodox writers are not. And what about those people who slide back and forth between denominations? For instance, G. K. Chesterton has a place in this book even though his *Orthodoxy* was written while he was still an Anglican. These are always judgment calls, but in general the overall trajectory of a person's life determined whether a book would be included here. In selecting these titles it is in no way suggested that Catholic books are somehow worthier than books written by Protestants, Orthodox, or, for that matter, by members of other faiths. It is because these "Catholic books" represent an identifiable religious tradition, however mixed that tradition may be, that they deserve to be together.

There are a few authors who were not Catholic but who are included because they wrote about Catholics or collaborated with Catholics on their books. John Neihardt was not a Catholic, but he wrote about Black Elk, who was. Simone Weil was never baptized because that remarkable woman feared church allegiance would undermine the solidarity she cherished with nonbelievers. Still, her writing was empowered by her belief in Catholic Christianity, so here she is.

To be in this volume a book has to be of interest to general readers. The contents gather a smattering of theology books, histories, a touch of philosophy, biography and autobiography, some poetry, a considerable amount of fiction, and a great deal of spiritual writing. These, hopefully, are books that people today can actually "read." There was some effort made to show the wide range of Catholic writing without loading the volume down with moral or systematic theology. Textbooks, reference books, and professional manuals are mostly excluded. Thomas Aquinas's *Summa Theologiae* is surely one of the greatest Catholic books, but who is going to pick it up and read it from beginning to end?

Similarly with the recent *Catechism of the Catholic Church*. However, Raymond Brown's *Introduction to the New Testament* is included to show the accomplishments of modern scripture scholarship. You may never read it through, but you will find Brown very readable. Also, the documents of Vatican II are included for the reason that one simply cannot understand contemporary Catholicism without them.

Our one hundred books are listed chronologically, according to the recorded year they were first published in their original language. Because the older titles were not published in the same sense that books are published since Gutenberg, the best the historical record can do is tell us (often only approximately) when an author completed his or her work.

Last of all, to be included here a title had to be available in printed form or online as this volume was written. The Book Notes at the end include information about editions and publishers. In some cases, where there are several editions of a particular title available, comparing certain editions seemed useful. Such comparisons are subjective and nonscholarly. They are simply the suggestions of one reader recommending books to a friend, nothing more.

Thanks are extended to the many people who encouraged and supported the preparation of this book. First among these is Jan-Erik Guerth of BlueBridge, who first suggested the idea to me and had faith that I could pull it off.

Thanks to my wife, Pat, who constantly encouraged me and spent hours discussing the books being reviewed. Her only concern was what I would work on when the book was finished. We'll see.

Thanks, too, to the helpful staff at the library of the General Theological Seminary in New York City; to Ned Coughlin, SJ;

Frank Stroud, SJ, of the DeMello Spirituality Center at Fordham University; to Steve Schoenig, SJ, for his insights on Tolkien; to Judith Walker, Christopher Eckl, Charles E. Curran, Lesley Ann Woo, Barbara Scheele, and Stacy Cavanaugh—all of whom made helpful suggestions; to my sons Chris and Ken who, when they were in New York, suffered my presence in their bedroom (my office); to Paulist Press, Templegate Press, ISI Books, Loyola Press, and OCD Press, all of which kindly made review copies available; and to many other friends, including Gil and Lynn Gordon, for their encouragement and support.

SAYINGS AND STORIES

(Fourth Century ◆ *Spirituality)*

THE DESERT FATHERS

(c. 325)

They had no intention of writing books or having books written about them. Many of them couldn't read or write anyway. Most of them just wanted to be left alone. As far as the rest of the world was concerned, these desert dwellers wanted to disappear. They wanted to die. That was the whole idea.

In the first centuries AD Christians did die by the thousands—put to death by despotic regimes for which Christianity was a subversive ideology. But then came the Edict of Milan. In 313 Emperor Constantine ended the persecution of Christians—in fact made Christianity the state religion. For three centuries Christians had proven their total faith in God by being martyred. Now they lacked the means to give themselves totally to God, so they died symbolically—by going into the desert.

The Desert Fathers (and Mothers, for their number included women) appeared predominantly in fourth-century Egypt, and most of the stories about them date to that time and place. Eventually, of course, the movement spread to the eastern shores of the Mediterranean and then moved with John Cassian and Egeria into Europe. But the original impulse was limited to North Africa, and especially to that region west of the Nile known as Scete. What these hermits did and said was passed down first through the oral tradition and later was recorded in Latin in the *Verba Seniorum* (Words of the Elders). That collection, and others, has been mined by writers and readers ever since.

So what are these stories? Some are only a single sentence—
"It was said of Abba Agatho that for three years he carried a stone
in his mouth until he learned to be silent."—while others are a
paragraph or more. Here is an example:

> "Once the Fathers in Scete asked Abba Moses to come to an
> assembly to judge the fault of a certain brother, but he refused.
> When they insisted, he took a basket that had a hole in it,
> filled it with sand, and carried it on his shoulders. When the
> Fathers saw him coming they asked him what the basket might
> mean. He answered, 'My sins run out behind me, and I do not
> see them, and I am come this day to judge failings which are
> not mine.'"

The sayings of the Desert Fathers are rarely moralistic because
the Fathers took such pains to avoid judging others. They are
instructive, wise, shrewd in their appreciation of human nature,
and occasionally humorous. The punch lines are unexpected. Like
Zen stories they often challenge us to see in ways we never saw
before.

The Desert Fathers and Mothers were true Christian radicals
who tried to live strictly according to the gospel. All other loyal-
ties—to family, to state, even to the church—were shucked off in
the desert sands. Commitment and simplicity were all. Perhaps
this is why these men and women, and their stories, continue to
fascinate and move believers even today.

THE LIFE OF ANTONY

(*c. 360* ✦ *Biography*)

ATHANASIUS

(*c. 295–373*)

It was the custom of Greeks to remember the lives of their heroes and write them down so that people of a later era would have models to emulate. So it was that when Christian monks from the East wished to learn more about the life of their precursor Antony, and how he lived and died, they asked Athanasius, the bishop of Alexandria, and he quickly composed a detailed account. What he wrote became the classic biography of Christian antiquity.

Antony (or Anthony) is considered the father of Christian monasticism. Born of wealthy parents around the year 250 in the Greek-Christian city of Alexandria, he one day heard the gospel message being read in church, "If you wish to be perfect, go, sell your possessions, and give the money to the poor, and you will have treasure in heaven; then come, follow me" (Mt 19:21). Antony immediately gave away all that he owned and went into the Egyptian desert to live as simply as possible. He prayed, he fasted, he contended with demons, he instructed other monks who sought enlightenment, he healed the ill who appeared at his doorstep. When he died (at the age of 104), his disciples buried his body secretly because Antony didn't want it revered as a relic.

Today's reader may feel that Antony's life was admirable but not really the stuff of a juicy biography. Athanasius didn't see it that way. The bishop—who was a formidable man in his day, being one of the movers and shakers at the Council of Nicaea in 325—had two aims in mind. First, because there wasn't a developed literature of asceticism during this era, Athanasius wanted to show what a holy life *looked like*. A holy life that didn't involve martyrdom, that is. Second, Athanasius wanted to counter the Arians—heretics condemned at Nicea who maintained that living a good life simply meant imitating Jesus who, himself, was merely a good man. In his *Life of Antony*, Athanasius portrays the path to perfection as spiritual warfare that advances slowly, step by step, and that can't be won without the active participation of Christ, the Son of God. A politician to his fingertips, Athanasius makes his theological points even as he tells a good story.

The Life of Antony is a readable work, short, fast moving, that has practical spiritual guidance to offer, even to contemporary believers. There are whole chapters relating instructions from Antony to his followers. These monologues are balanced by miracle stories, or delicious incidents (like the time Antony walked through a river of crocodiles), or accounts of the saint wrestling with demons. Anyone who has ever dealt with temptation knows what that's about.

Athanasius rejoices that Antony "is famous everywhere . . . and is dearly missed by people who never saw him." He adds that even though such Christian heroes "act in secret and may want to be forgotten, nevertheless the Lord shows them like lamps to everyone, so that those who hear may know that the commandments have power for amendment of life, and may gain zeal for the way of virtue."

THE CONFESSIONS

(c. 398 ✦ Autobiography)

AUGUSTINE OF HIPPO

(354–430)

Augustine wrote his famous *Confessions* a decade after he had converted to Christianity and shortly after he had become bishop of Hippo in North Africa. He was troubled and casting around for some way to exercise his new role as teacher of the Christian community—being so new to the faith himself—when it occurred to him he could do it by telling his own story. This is how the first great work of autobiography in the Christian era came to be written.

Except that it is really not an autobiography at all. Certainly it is not a gossipy confession of the sort turned out by today's celebrities. The *Confessions* is a book of teaching with elements of a story carefully arranged to bring the unbeliever to the truth of the Christian faith. According to Garry Wills, "The whole work, and not just the final books, is a theological work, a preparation for the reading of Scriptures. . . ."

Consider the famous conversion scene in Book Eight of *The Confessions* that takes place in a garden. Commentators have pointed out the similarities of this garden with biblical gardens, especially Eden and Gethsemane. In Augustine's account he is tormented by indecision as he sits in the garden with his friend Alypius. He weeps, he thrashes about, his "very bones cried out." He goes apart from Alypius and hears a childlike voice command, "Take and read." Rushing back to his friend, Augustine snatches up the scriptures that open to a passage instructing him to "give up reveling and drunkenness" (Romans 13:13). It is the sign Augustine had been waiting for. He is converted.

Long before that event, however, Augustine had found other ways to extract Christian truth from his life story. "Even in my infancy," he writes, "I was doing something that deserved blame." In other words, he was sinful from birth. Augustine practically invented the doctrine of original sin—a holdover, some maintain, from his Manichaean days.

This is not to say these *Confessions* are all fiction. They generally recount Augustine's life. They acknowledge his sinful youth, his flirtation with the Manichaeans, the influences of his mother, Monica, and St. Ambrose. But the work is not autobiography in the sense we use that word today.

Augustine was a great rhetorician—one who has mastered the art of argument. His book is a magnificent argument. He presents it in the form of a prayer, written not for us but for God. We just listen in as he confesses to God, acknowledges his sin, and gives an account of his faith.

Because of its language and because Augustine is one of the great shapers of Christianity, *The Confessions* remains a powerful and moving book. His memorable words to God resonate like the psalms:

"The closed heart does not shut out your eye, and man's hardness cannot resist your hand."

"I pray that I may find grace before you so that the inner secrets of your words may be laid open to me when I knock."

"You have made us for yourself, and our hearts are restless until they rest in you."

CONFERENCES

(c. 426 ✦ Spirituality)

JOHN CASSIAN

(c. 360–c. 435)

John Cassian is listed here between the Desert Fathers and Benedict, which fairly describes his place in the history of Christian spirituality. Cassian was a bridge figure who brought the traditions of the Desert Fathers to Europe. Benedict read him. So did Anselm in the eleventh century and John Main in the twentieth. His *Conferences* were a conscious effort to pass along the wisdom of the desert to men and women who came to monasticism from very different backgrounds and cultures.

As far as we know, Cassian was born somewhere east of the Mediterranean, perhaps in Romania, and was trained in Latin and Greek. As a young monk he lived for a time in Bethlehem, then went to Egypt to learn from the monks there. He later spent time in Constantinople and Rome, moving finally to southern Gaul where Christians were beginning to experiment with communal living. He founded a community for men in Marseilles and was associated with other groups of men and women in Provence. He was the bearer of tradition. They looked to him for guidance.

Cassian was dealing with individuals who desired to do something great for God but weren't sure how to go about it. Like neophytes everywhere, they wanted to be saints overnight. They needed encouragement, but they also needed to be reined back. The road to perfection is a long road, and windy. So Cassian preached the necessity for "purity of heart"—the rectitude of intention, unsullied by anger, self-interest, or ambition. It wasn't sanctity, but it was something his monks could work on. According to Cassian, "For its sake we hold family, country, honors, riches, the delight of this world and indeed all pleasure in low esteem, and we do so always to hold on to purity of heart."

There was the question, too, of obeying Paul's command to "pray always." Some monasteries met the command by filling the day's schedule with liturgical prayer. Cassian, though, insisted that his monks practice recollection instead. For times when they drifted off, he gave them a scripture verse to recite, "Come to my help, O God; Lord, hurry to my rescue." It was the first recommended use of a mantra in the Roman church.

Cassian wrote these *Conferences* himself but presented them as if he were sitting at the feet of the great Desert Fathers taking dictation. The twenty-four conferences cover such themes as discretion, prayer, sin, chastity, spiritual knowledge, and the way to perfection.

Reading the *Conferences* today, one appreciates the greatness of heart and pastoral concern of the author. As a guide to spirituality, he may seem esoteric to contemporary Christians—being of interest primarily to monks or students of spirituality. Yet Cassian has things to teach us. Like his monks, we all need reminding at times to put God above all things, to become more like Mary of Bethany who sought to listen, and less like Martha with her worrying and running about.

"To cling always to God and to the things of God—this must be our major effort," says Cassian; "this must be the road that the heart follows unswervingly."

THE RULE OF ST. BENEDICT

(c. 530 ✦ Spirituality)

BENEDICT OF NURSIA

(c. 480–c. 547)

There is only one "book of the church"—the Holy Bible. The Bible is so obviously the book of the Christian faith that it would be presumptuous to include it in this collection. Yet if one had to name a second "book of the church"—a book that has shaped and given life to Catholic Christianity over the centuries—it would be *The Rule of St. Benedict.* This short volume of advice and instruction, written for monks in the sixth century, gave a trajectory to spirituality that the church has never lost. It colors the way Catholics still live for the community, their attitude toward possessions, they way they balance prayer and work, their view of authority, and their attitudes toward welcoming outsiders.

Reading the rule today, one does not encounter high-flown theology on one hand or unctuous piety on the other. It is a practical book, simply written. True, it describes a way of life that no longer exists the way it did 1,500 years ago. Contemporary Benedictines do not observe every letter of it. But the heart of the rule still captures the essence of the committed life. Soberly and without fanfare it lays out a way of living together that can bring people to sanctity.

Benedict of Nursia is generally considered the father of Western monasticism. He adapted the spiritual practice of solitary hermits, popular in North Africa, and founded monasteries of monks living together in *coenobia*, or communities. But precisely *how* would they live? Here was Benedict's genius: monks would devote themselves to the good of the whole, under obedience to an abbot.

What they would eat, how they would sleep, the manner of their prayer, the way abbots would be chosen—everything is laid out in the rule.

Scholars aren't positive that Benedict actually wrote all or any of it. The earliest known manuscript of the rule dates from the ninth century, three hundred years after the saint's death. In addition, the text borrows from other rules extant in the Eastern church—from the writings of Pachomius and Basil, both in the fourth century, and from the anonymous *Rule of the Master* that antedated Benedict.

Yet *The Rule of St. Benedict* is a synthesis that far transcends its sources. It was written at a time when the social and political order was crumbling. Seventy years before Benedict was born in the city, Visigoths sacked Rome. By the time he died Lombards were threatening the city again. Italy and all of Europe were in disarray. Yet within the walls of monasteries that lived according to the rule there was order, civility, industry, and even a measure of democracy. Benedict's rule describes a church that even today is the church of our dearest hopes.

PRAYERS AND MEDITATIONS

(c. 1075 ✦ Spirituality)

ANSELM OF CANTERBURY

(c. 1033–1109)

Anselm was one of the most famous churchmen of his age. He was a philosopher (one of the fathers of medieval Scholasticism), an author whose prayers and letters reached all over Europe, and a pastor and administrator—the abbot of Bec monastery in Normandy and later archbishop of Canterbury. Anselm was a towering figure, a Renaissance man before the Renaissance.

Anselm did much to change the way people prayed in the Middle Ages. Before his time, when people felt called to prayer they went to church or took up their Book of Hours containing psalms and liturgical prayers. Anselm himself was nurtured in the Benedictine tradition and therefore was intimately familiar with the public formulas of prayer. Beginning at this time, however, people were beginning to imagine prayer as a personal, private devotion, using words that were not in the public texts. Anselm modeled what such private prayer should be like. His prayers are humble and ardent, buttressed by good theology and scripture.

Anselm composed his prayers while still at Bec and sent them by mail or messenger to friends and monastic colleagues. Most of the prayers are directed to a scriptural figure: there are prayers to God, to Christ, to Mary, to John the Baptist, St. Peter and St. Paul, to John the Evangelist. In addition he wrote a famous prayer to the Holy Cross and one to be said before receiving Holy Communion.

The carefully constructed prayers were intended to lift the one praying out of an apathetic state and inspire him or her to consider

God's loving care. They are often marked by wordplay typical of medieval writers. For instance, the Prayer to the Holy Cross notes that evil men employed the cross

> ". . . that they might kill life;
> he [Jesus] that he might destroy death.
> They that they might condemn the Savior;
> he that he might save the condemned.
> They that they might bring death to the living;
> he to bring life to the dead."

His prayer to Christ is significant because prior to this time the church, as a reaction to Arianism, encouraged the faithful to address all prayers to the First Person of the Trinity. Anselm, though, felt himself drawn powerfully to Christ in a way that anticipates Ignatius Loyola. Passionately he declares, "I thirst for you, I hunger for you, I desire you, I sigh for you, I covet you: I am like an orphan . . . who, weeping and wailing, does not cease to cling to the dear face with his whole heart."

Benedicta Ward's contemporary edition of Anselm's prayers also contains the *Proslogion* (allocution) that expresses his famous ontological argument for God's existence. To Anselm God is "that which nothing greater can be thought." He does not offer this as a "proof" of God's existence, since for Anselm we can come to God only by faith; but it is a way of going deeper into God's mystery—a way of faith seeking understanding. It is Anselm's contribution to the great awakening of medieval philosophy, and it has reverberated down through history, influencing many later thinkers, including Karl Barth in the twentieth century. The *Proslogion* is delicately articulated and is itself a prayer that rises up out of a great man's faith.

THE LETTERS

(c. 1130 ✦ Biography)

PETER ABELARD *(1079–1142)* and HELOISE *(c. 1101–c. 1164)*

My heart was not in me but with you. Now, even more, if it is not with you it is nowhere. Truly, without you it cannot exist."

These are not the words of a nun writing about God. This is a nun writing to her former lover, her former husband.

". . . The love I have always borne you, as everyone knows, [is] a love which is beyond all bounds."

And indeed, everyone did know. It was common gossip at the time. All of Paris knew of the scandalous love between Peter Abelard, the famous teacher and philosopher, and Heloise (or Héloïse), the niece of a Parisian church official. He was thirty-nine. She was seventeen. When people threatened to put a stop to it, Abelard fled with Heloise to his home in Brittany and there married her.

Too late. The scandal engulfed them anyway. When they returned to Paris, a gang of thugs broke into Abelard's lodgings and castrated him. Heloise was forced to enter the convent. He became a monk.

Now, many years later, they are corresponding again.

"God knows I never sought anything in you except yourself," she writes. "I wanted simply you, nothing of yours. I looked for no marriage bond, no marriage portion, and it was not my own pleasures and wishes I sought to gratify, as you well know, but yours."

He responds, urging her to find consolation in her religious state: "Seek piety in this at least, lest you cut yourself off from me who am hastening, you believe, toward God."

Peter Abelard was the foremost philosopher in twelfth-century Europe. He specialized in "dialectic"—a combination of logic and rhetoric that formed the basis of medieval liberal arts education. Students flocking to him from all countries made Paris the first great university town in Europe. But he was a contentious man. Not only did he lose his head over Heloise, he made enemies by the way he dominated philosophical opponents. When he became an abbot, his own monks tried to poison him. Eventually he tangled with Bernard of Clairvaux, a powerful man with very different theological sensibilities. Abelard's writings were condemned. His academic career was ruined.

Of Heloise we know much less—not even her last name. The little we know suggests she was also a very remarkable person. She was the foundress of a convent, a considerable linguist, and, according to Peter the Venerable, "wholly devoted to philosophy in the true sense."

She also knew what she wanted. When Abelard died, she had his body brought to her convent for burial so that when she died, she could be interred beside him.

Most editions of *The Letters of Abelard and Heloise* open with Abelard's *Historia calamitatum* ("The Story of My Troubles") that provides the background for the letters. The letters themselves are of two kinds—"personal" letters between the lovers, and "letters of direction" in which Abelard offers guidance to Heloise and her nuns.

SCIVIAS

(1152 ✦ Spirituality)

HILDEGARD OF BINGEN
(1098–1179)

People have called Hildegard of Bingen one of the most remarkable, fascinating, original women of the Middle Ages. She was all of that. She was an abbess, a seer, writer, composer, preacher, herbalist, church reformer, advisor to bishops and popes, and—not the least of her honors—a holy woman. Blessed Hildegard's feast day is celebrated in Germany on September 17.

From earliest childhood this daughter of a knight experienced visions. She saw strange lights with people in them and sometimes heard voices. (People have since theorized the phenomena were brought on by migraines.) But, since Hildegard was clearly a bright, pious child, she was placed in a monastery as handmaid to a recluse. The two women drew others around them. Years later, when the older woman died, the nuns chose Hildegard as their abbess.

Hildegard had no formal schooling, but religious superiors encouraged her to record her visions, which she did in her most famous book, known today as *Scivias*. The word comes from the longer Latin title *Scito Vias Domini*: Know the Ways of the Lord. Their authenticity was vouched for by no less than Bernard of Clairvaux and Pope Eugenius III.

What did the visions say? They contained no startling revelations but summed up a great deal of doctrinal and commonsense teaching ranging from the Trinity and the Fall and Salvation to the sacraments and moral virtues. Some of the issues are practical: Can stars foretell the future? (No.) May a husband and wife make love during pregnancy? (Absolutely not.) Mostly the visions served to support the church and its teachings against independent rulers and the new monied class.

"If Hildegard had been a male theologian," says one commentator, "her *Scivias* would undoubtedly have been considered one of the most important early medieval summas." And this is crucial: Here was a woman instructing a male-dominated society what to believe and how to behave, calling priests back to celibacy, husbands to faithfulness, the church to holiness. The fact that this instruction was claimed to originate in heavenly "visions" made it awkward, even impossible, for men to discount it.

Hildegard never lacked energy or political acumen. She leveraged her convent away from a men's monastery and made it independent. She composed plainchant (still sung today), started gardens, and wrote about the medicinal powers of plants and soil. People came from great distances to consult with her on all sorts of subjects. At the age of sixty she began preaching in Rhineland churches and public squares, and continued to do so for another twelve years.

Scivias was her book for the ages. Actually Hildegard herself was a work for the ages.

PARZIVAL

(c. 1205 ✦ Poetry)

WOLFRAM VON ESCHENBACH

(c. 1170–c. 1220)

The search for the Holy Grail is one of the oldest and most persistent legends of the Christian tradition. In the popular mind the Grail is connected with stories surrounding King Arthur and his knights, but it has roots that go back further in time than that—to Persia and Spain, to ancient harvest rites and fertility cults, to a mysterious Fisher King who lies wounded, waiting for a word that will heal him and his kingdom. T. S. Eliot alludes to this older tradition in his poem "The Waste Land."

The person who first tried to set down the Grail legend in a systematic way (sometime before the year 1190) was Chrétien de Troyes, a French poet. However his recounting of "Perceval" and his search for the "Graal" was left unfinished. Next was Wolfram von Eschenbach, a Bavarian knight attached to the court of the Landgrave of Thuringia. Wolfram's *Parzival* was probably written in the years after 1200 and borrowed from Chrétien and from other sources. It became the primary channel for the story that flowed down the years to Thomas Malory, Sir Walter Scott, Richard Wagner, Lerner & Lowe, and even to Monty Python.

In von Eschenbach's retelling, the Grail is not the chalice of the Last Supper but a mysterious stone that fell from the heavens, and which is given fresh power each Good Friday by an angel with a consecrated host. This Grail stone is the property of the Fisher King who lies gravely wounded in a castle protected by Grail knights. The stone keeps the king from dying, but it can't heal him. Only a visiting knight who asks the right question can do that.

Parzival is a young knight just learning his craft and the ways of chivalry. The epic poem gives considerable space to his forebears and early adventures. There are jousts with other knights, damsels rescued. He possesses a magic sword. He is instructed by a sorceress. At one point Parzival meets Anfortas, the Fisher King, but, being inexperienced, he fails to ask the right question. So the king continues to suffer, and his kingdom with him.

The bulk of von Eschenbach's tale is devoted to the search by Parzival and his fellow knight Gawan (Gawain) for the Grail. They travel through strange lands that could be Spain or the Middle East or Wales—one is never sure which. They actually meet King Arthur and become members of the Round Table. Parzival is reunited with a long-lost brother, Feirefiz. At last he encounters Anfortas again and this time asks the right question—which is an inquiry about the older man's health as a sign of compassion. The Fisher King is healed, and Parzival becomes the new Lord of the Grail.

In Medieval German *Parzival* is accounted as poetry, but the version available to English readers is a prose text, and very lengthy prose at that. The translation tends toward archaic usage, for instance using the word "puissant" for "mighty." When reading it you should keep at your elbow a good commentary that explores the myths behind the story. Still, the Grail legend is an archetypal account of our spiritual quest for wholeness and maturity, and von Eschenbach's *Parzival* the masterful creation of an ideal knight as servant of God and humanity.

THE SOUL'S JOURNEY INTO GOD

(1259 ◆ Spirituality)

BONAVENTURE

(1221–1274)

Bonaventure, the eminent Franciscan of the thirteenth century, was both a philosopher and theologian. He was one of the great figures of the High Middle Ages, ranking alongside Aquinas in influence. But while Aquinas was a follower of Aristotle whose world consisted of real objects and perceptions, Bonaventure was influenced by Plato who believed the world is a reflection of a greater, preexisting principle, which in Bonaventure's terms meant God. It bore God's fingerprints and shone with God's being. The great Franciscan felt himself surrounded by Divinity, and this belief inflamed his writing with mystical intensity.

Bonaventure's most enduring work is *The Soul's Journey into God*, composed when he was minister-general of the Franciscans. As he tells the story, he had gone to pray on Mount La Verna in Tuscany—the place where Francis of Assisi's hands and feet were pierced by an angel. He was reflecting on that event when it occurred to him that the angel's six wings symbolized the six steps of a soul's ascent to God. Struck by the elegance of the idea, Bonaventure immediately began composing *The Soul's Journey*, a brief work with a prologue and seven chapters.

Chapters one and two explore our ascent to God in nature—always a popular Franciscan theme. We find God in the universe and in objects that we taste, touch, hear, and smell. The next two chapters consider the greater human powers—memory, intellect, will—and powers that have been graciously given to us, such as the word of God in scripture and infused contemplation. Chapters five and six consider God's own self, viewed under the aspects of Being and Good. Bonaventure's treatment is an extended meditation on the Trinity in which the Three Persons are coexistent and yet diffuse.

The soul passes through these six stages on its journey to perfection just as the world passed through six days of creation. Then on the seventh we possess "desire not understanding . . . God not man, darkness not clarity, not light but fire that totally inflames us and carries us into God . . ."

This is a mystical treatise, not a manual of the spiritual life. Bonaventure's *Journey* is like an idealized landscape of creation, with God in one place and humans in another, described in such a way that the path humans must follow becomes intelligible.

It is a work that can be read at several levels. One can ignore the philosophy and approach it just for spiritual nourishment, in which case Bonaventure's ardor provides ample inspiration. Even then, though, *The Soul's Journey into God* needs to be read slowly, and at any level it is helpful to have a good commentary.

In Latin the work is known as *Itinerarium mentis in Deum*, often translated as "The Mind's Journey to God." However, Ewert Cousins, an authority on Bonaventure, maintains that *mens* is an indefinite word that sometimes means "mind" and sometimes "soul." Whichever way you take it, the word alludes to the most profound depths of the human person.

THE LITTLE FLOWERS OF
ST. FRANCIS OF ASSISI

(c. 1275 ✦ Spirituality)

UGOLINO DI MONTE SANTA MARIA

(Thirteenth Century)

Francis of Assisi died in 1226 and was canonized two years later—leaping almost immediately from simple holy man to near-mythic saint. The official biography written soon after his death by Thomas of Celano and Bonaventure set forth the known facts of his life, but somehow legends and memories of Francis outpaced written history. He was just too big to fit between the covers of a single book.

There was another problem: as soon as Francis was gone, different factions within the Franciscan order laid claim to his memory. Those known as the *spirituales* argued that Francis's primitive rule should govern the lives of all Franciscans, while the *relaxati* under Elias of Crotona, a companion of Francis and later minister-general of the order, favored a more accommodating rule allowing Franciscans to own property. The split was not sorted out until Bonaventure became minister-general in 1257 and established a new rule leaning toward the *spirituales*. But even then, Bonaventure ordered the destruction of all writings on Francis so that only the official version would survive.

Throughout this period memories of Francis endured. Stories were passed from friar to friar, generation to generation. When eventually those brothers who knew the man from Assisi during his lifetime were beginning to pass away, there was a new effort to collect stories about him. This was accomplished by a friar named Ugolino di Monte Santa Maria, about whom we know almost nothing. Originally called the *Actus beati Francisci et sociorum ejus*, the collection became better known as the *Fioretti*, or "Little Flowers" of St. Francis. The work was translated and copied in many editions. Different versions arranged the accounts in different sequences, editing and amending them. It was a living tradition.

It is only in these *Fioretti* that we find most of the popular legends that grew up around Francis of Assisi: how he preached to the birds, how he tamed the wolf of Gubbio and made nests for the wild doves. The stories are short, charming, often funny—like the time Francis sent Brother Bernard into town to preach dressed only in his underwear, until, feeling bad about it, Francis stripped down to *his* underwear and followed Bernard. We are told the laughter at Bernard's expense died away, and that many in town were converted that day.

People have remarked on the "childlike artlessness" of the *Fioretti*. They were wildly popular in the fourteenth and fifteenth centuries, and they continue to amuse and move us even today.

Are they true? Did they really happen? There may be some truth to them—one can't know for sure; but certainly they truly reflect the simplicity of the Franciscan ideal. The very naiveté of these folk tales serves to remind us that holiness need not be complicated. Loving God basically comes down to letting go of all that is *not* God. What could be simpler, or more Franciscan, than that?

THE DIVINE COMEDY

(c. 1310 ✦ Poetry)

DANTE ALIGHIERI
(1265–1321)

He was a poet who created a new epic blending current events, historical characters, and his own friends, all preserved in a matrix of visionary mysticism and captured in a vigorous blend of dialects, including his native Tuscan, with such beauty and grace that the Italian language could be said to date from his writing.

He was a politician who at a young age became one of the ruling magistrates of Florence until an emissary of the pope betrayed his party and exiled him forever from the city, smashing all political hopes, so that—embittered and lonely—only in his imagination could he construct a truly just place where virtue is rewarded and evil punished.

He was a middle-aged man who found himself without direction in a dark forest (not uncommon for middle-aged males) with wild animals threatening his way, when suddenly he met a mentor who took him in hand, led him into dark places where he could speak with the dead and move step-by-step back into the light.

He was Dante Alighieri, whose great work, *The Divine Comedy*, magnificently layers all these scenarios and which has become, over the centuries, *the* great Christian epic. The *Commedia*, as Dante called it, is really three long poems broken up into cantos (songs) that describe his transit of hell, purgatory, and heaven, initially with the guidance of the Latin poet Virgil and then under the care of Beatrice Portinari, an idealized Florentine woman Dante had worshiped since childhood.

Not only great literature, the *Commedia* skillfully uses insights from Thomas Aquinas, Pseudo-Dionysius, Bonaventure, and Bernard in a way that makes it a kind of Renaissance *Summa*. Dante had a sophisticated theological sensibility.

With all of these layers and contextualizations, one cannot read Dante's great work without a good commentary to track the many biblical, classical, and medieval personalities, landscapes, myths, time systems, and theology. Most editions have notes either at the bottoms of pages or at the end of each canto.

The Divine Comedy is more popular in our own day than it ever was, aided by Dante societies in many cities, by ongoing scholarship, and greatly benefiting from newer and more splendid translations. The first task for any translator is to decide whether to keep or abandon Dante's three-line rhyme scheme. Henry Wadsworth Longfellow and Dorothy L. Sayers kept it; of the recent translations, John Ciardi, Allen Mandelbaum, Mark Musa, and Robert Durling abandoned it, but gave the epic a vigorous modern style.

SERMONS

(c. 1315 ✦ Spirituality)

MEISTER ECKHART

(c. 1260–c. 1328)

It may seem odd to have a great book that is not really a book but a collection of sermons. Eckhart von Hochheim, universally known as Meister Eckhart, wrote no books in the modern sense of that word, yet his writings were so influential in his own day—and suddenly again in ours—that it is impossible to ignore him. Eckhart is one of the most famous and controversial mystical theologians in the Catholic tradition. His contributions to literature are found in his sermons and in a few tracts written during his life.

Eckhart was part of the enormous flowering of learning that accompanied the founding of the Dominican order in the later Middle Ages. He was born only forty years after the death of the order's founder, Dominic Guzman, in 1221, and his lifetime overlapped the lives of the Dominicans Albert the Great and Thomas Aquinas. He held positions of responsibility in his order and taught at Paris, Strasbourg, and Cologne. In addition to scholarly lectures he preached sermons to uneducated believers.

And what sermons they were! Eckhart's preaching was calculated to challenge the listener and upset religious complacency. "What is life?" asked Eckhart at one point. "God's being is my life. If my life is God's being, then God's existence must be my existence and God is-ness is my is-ness" (Sermon 6). Eckhart believed the indwelling Spirit so takes over the soul of the humble person that the two share one being. This is not a metaphor, Eckhart insisted, but a fact: "What is changed into something else becomes one with it. I am so changed into [God] that he produces his being in me as one, not just similar. By the living God this is true! There is no distinction. . . . God and I, we are one" (Sermon 6).

Later he said, "This is how a man acts when he thinks he can flee from God, and yet he cannot flee from him; every corner where he may go, reveals God to him. He thinks that he is fleeing God, and he runs into [God's] lap. God bears his Only Begotten Son in you, whether you like it or not" (Sermon 22).

Eckhart was not a systematic theologian but a mystical theologian who sought to explain the mystery of God's union with the soul. However, as one might expect, putting every holy person on the level of God's Son was abhorrent to some church leaders. The archbishop of Cologne accused Eckhart of heresy; Pope John XXII issued a letter specifically condemning several of Eckhart's statements. Personally the preacher was never found guilty of heresy. Before the issue was fully resolved, he died.

Recent years have seen a recovery of Eckhart's writing and ideas. Contemporary readers admire him for the Zen-like quality of his insights. Both Rudolf Otto and D. T. Suzuki have remarked on similarities between Eckhart and Buddhist mystics. He is esteemed in Germany as the first writer of speculative prose to abandon Latin and write in German. In 1985 even Pope John Paul II quoted him approvingly.

In his day and ours, Meister Eckhart was and is a unique voice with a unique approach to mystical experience. He continues to upset religious complacency. His sermons speak for themselves.

THE CLOUD OF UNKNOWING

(c. 1367 ◆ Spirituality)

ANONYMOUS

(Fourteenth Century)

The very title of this book is unsettling. That no one knows who wrote it adds to its mystery. The author makes no pretense of reaching out to a mass readership. In fact he says in *The Cloud's* prologue that it is not for everybody. It's a book for specialists, then, yet a book that has been read and treasured for seven hundred years.

The Cloud of Unknowing follows the *via negativa* (negative path) that approaches God from the blind side—not God's blind side but our own. It assumes that because we cannot really know God we should set aside our intellect and imagination and simply rest in silence before God's mystery. Like Moses who entered a cloud at the top of Mount Sinai, people find God obscured even when they approach in prayer. Or, as this author says,

> "This darkness and cloud is always between you and your God, no matter what you do, and it prevents you from seeing him clearly by the light of understanding in your reason, and experiencing him in sweetness of love in your affection. So set yourself to rest in this darkness as long as you can, always crying out after him whom you love."

Is there any hope for prayer? *The Cloud of Unknowing* maintains there is. Although the intellect cannot attain God, love can pierce the cloud and provide an intimate connection with the Holy One. You don't have to beat your breast and proclaim your wretchedness—love erases all that. You don't have to *do* anything—just be with God. Love, all by itself, can transport us more deeply into God's embrace than active prayer can ever do.

Such a simple method! Why don't more people follow it? First, it requires considerable self-discipline. Much of *The Cloud of Unknowing* focuses on developing the inner virtues of humility, self-knowledge, and perseverance that are preconditions for this meditative kind of prayer. Second, the method takes time—something today's busy spiritual seekers don't always have. *The Cloud* was written for contemplative monks (probably by a Cistercian living in the British Midlands). They could devote hours each day over a period of months and years to developing their prayer lives. Even in our own day this sort of prayer is more prevalent inside monasteries than outside.

As a book, however, *The Cloud of Unknowing* is neither arcane nor difficult to grasp. It consists of seventy-five brief chapters, most of them just a page or two long. It was originally written in Middle English that was remarkably clear and easy to read, and most of the available modern English translations retain that clarity. People who are serious about deepening their relationship with God or who are curious about the way others have attempted it should at least look at *The Cloud of Unknowing*. For all of its initial mysteriousness, it is an accessible classic that brings light to the dark side of prayer.

THE DIALOGUE

(1377 ✦ Spirituality)

CATHERINE OF SIENA

(1347–1380)

Catherine of Siena lived during the first bloom of the Italian Renaissance, before the Borgias ruled Rome or the Medicis Florence. The medieval social order was crumbling, but there was no clear sense of what was coming next. The popes were under the thumb of the French king and resided in Avignon. The Black Death was ravaging Europe. The city-states of northern Italy were in disarray, constantly warring, yet were beginning to enjoy new prosperity based on trade with the East. It was an unsettled time that cried out for order—and Catherine of Siena tried to provide it through her writing and by the sheer magnetism of her personality.

Catherine was the twenty-fourth of twenty-five children, the daughter of a lower-middle-class tradesman in Siena. She was drawn to religious life at a very young age, taking the habit of a Dominican tertiary at the age of sixteen and living as an anchorite in a room in her parents' house. A few years later she received a message during prayer telling her to get involved in worldly matters, so she left her cell, rejoined her family, and began a letter-writing campaign to government and church leaders, including Pope Gregory XI.

Catherine seemed to have a magnetic presence. A crowd of disciples, many of them men, used to follow her through the streets of Siena and invade her family's home. State and church officials who received her letters wanted to meet this high-spirited young woman who gave them such blunt advice. In this way her public life was launched.

Catherine's successful efforts to restore the papacy to Rome have been recorded elsewhere. Less known are her writings, her letters, and particularly *The Dialogue*, which Catherine called "my book." She dictated it in 1377–78, some say while rapt in prayer, since the book takes the form of an ecstatic dialogue between herself and God. However, it is a calculated work that patiently develops its subjects of personal sanctity and church reform. Her great theme was the joining of heart and mind—both love and truth—in the pursuit of holiness. In this way Catherine stands between the Middle Ages and the Renaissance: she endorsed the pious enthusiasm of the Middle Ages (heart) but insisted that it be nourished by the new learning of the Renaissance (mind). She further reflected the Renaissance by insisting on the need for knowing oneself: "A soul . . . [must] become accustomed to dwelling in the cell of self-knowledge in order to know better God's goodness toward her. . . ."

Recent scholarship has made *The Dialogue* more accessible by restoring its original structure. Still, it takes time to accustom oneself to the literary form—unfamiliar to modern readers—and Catherine's elaborate use of allegory. The various sections deal with such themes as the way of perfection, tears (i.e., holy emotion), truth, the mystical body of the church, providence, and obedience. The central section of the work envisions Christ as The Bridge who brings us straight to God the Father.

Catherine was a mystic but also a teacher who had an intense desire to lift up the people of her time. Exhausted by work and austerities, she died at the age of thirty-three—all of her candles burned out. Yet her great work, *The Dialogue*, remains.

THE CANTERBURY TALES

(c. 1387 ◆ Poetry)

GEOFFREY CHAUCER

(c. 1340–1400)

It may be surprising to find *The Canterbury Tales* included in a collection of great Catholic books. After all, Chaucer's band of pilgrims on the road to a shrine in Canterbury during the Middle Ages is made up mostly of drunks, grasping merchants, and worldly clerics, along with a few normal folk. And the tales they tell along the way are, in turns, calculating, bawdy, anti-Semitic, and self-serving. Are these supposed to be people of faith?

Well, yes. Like any great work of literature, *The Canterbury Tales* offers a picture of people busy being themselves. The device of making them accidental fellow travelers—and aren't we all?—allows Chaucer to show a cross-section of the society he knew. His party includes a knight, a prioress, a farmer, a merchant, a student, a widow (five times over), and many others—including Chaucer himself. We have detailed descriptions of each. We see what they are wearing; we hear how they speak.

Yet, while rich in detail, the portraits are complex and ambiguous. The gentleman knight was really a hired killer during the Hundred Years War. The pardoner tells a story of sudden, violent death, then follows it with a pitch for his Vatican-approved indulgences. Pardoners were the insurance agents of the Middle Ages.

The characters lean toward caricatures, but not malicious ones. As C. S. Lewis pointed out, "One can only parody a poem one admires." Elaborating on the point, W. H. Auden went on to say, "One can only blaspheme if one believes. The world of laughter is much more closely related to the world of worship and prayer than either is to the everyday, secular world of work. . . ."

So *The Canterbury Tales* is a religious work in the broad sense of that word. It still makes fine reading, even today. While it takes expertise to muddle through the Middle English original, there are fine translations into modern English available. The poetry lends itself to reading aloud; mouth the words to yourself as you go along. Notice how the meter and rhyme scheme change from character to character. Enjoy the way the pilgrims interrupt each other and argue over the meaning of the stories they tell.

Geoffrey Chaucer was in a good position to observe the society of his day. The son of a wine merchant, he was well connected at the English court, serving successively as a page, a soldier (captured, then ransomed, in France), a courtier, an ambassador, and a customs officer. During all this time he was writing poetry. *The Canterbury Tales* was the work of his mature years and was still unfinished at his death. He is buried in Westminster Abbey, the first of those interred in what is now called the Poets' Corner.

Each of the twenty-four tales told on the way to Canterbury contains its moral lesson. We are invited to take these with a grain of salt, but to take them. We could do worse than to follow the business advice of the canon's yeoman, for example, who claims:

"[If you] make God your adversary for a whim
And work at what is contrary to Him
And to His will, . . . you will never thrive
Though you transmute as long as you're alive.
Aye, there's the point for which my tale began,
And may God prosper every honest man!"

REVELATIONS OF DIVINE LOVE

(c. 1393 ♦ Spirituality)

JULIAN OF NORWICH

(c. 1342–c. 1416)

Julian of Norwich lived alone in a stone hut built against the walls of the parish church of St. Julian in the Conisford neighborhood of Norwich, England. While the original hut has disappeared—leveled during a bombing raid in World War II—we know it was small and had two windows: one giving access to the church interior and one facing out onto the street. During her lifetime people would stop there to seek advice from the famous anchoress who never left her cell.

There, in May 1373, so sick she was "on the point of death," Julian experienced a series of sixteen visions—"showings," as she called them—that greatly comforted her. When she regained her health she wrote two accounts of the experiences, first a short version and then, when she had a chance to reflect on their meaning, a longer version. Julian and her two texts were neglected in the centuries that followed. In our own day, however, they have become the subject of enormous interest and have made Julian one of the most famous of the medieval mystics.

The interest is surprising on the face of it because these *Revelations of Divine Love* can be a chore for modern readers. Julian used allegory, which is not a popular literary device today. And the *Revelations* are more theological than, for instance, *The Cloud of Unknowing*, a work from the same era and region.

Her popularity arises from the fact that Julian explored themes that are important and current today. Writing in a troubled age of war, incipient heresy, and rampant plague, Julian's God is not judging or punishing but one who "wraps and enfolds us with love" as if he were our clothing, a God "who is so tender that he may never desert us." According to Julian,

"[God] showed me something small, no bigger than a hazelnut, lying in the palm of my hand. . . . I looked at it with the eye of my understanding and I thought: What can this be? I was amazed that it could last, for I thought that because of its littleness it would suddenly have fallen into nothing. And I was answered in my understanding: It lasts and always will, because God loves it; and thus everything has being through the love of God."

Julian's God treats his subjects with loving gentleness. Should we fall into sin, then "our courteous Lord, touching us, moves and protects us." He desires that we see our sin "and meekly to acknowledge it; but he does not want us to remain there . . . He waits for us continually, moaning and mourning until we come [to him], for we are his joy and his delight. . . ."

Julian was not the first to draw attention to the motherliness of God, but she did it more extensively than any other medieval writer, even speaking of "our heavenly Mother Jesus." Her approach to God was strongly Trinitarian. In her view feminine qualities penetrated not just the Spirit but all three Persons.

The year of her death is not recorded. Perhaps she died in her cell during a plague year when death was everywhere. But even as she disappears from history she reminds us that "all will be well, and all manner of things will be well."

THE IMITATION OF CHRIST

(c. 1418 ✦ Spirituality)

THOMAS À KEMPIS

(c. 1380–1471)

John Wesley translated it into English. Ignatius Loyola read it every day. Pope John Paul I was reading it when he died. Thérèse of Lisieux at the age of fourteen had the book nearly memorized: name a chapter and she would recite it.

The book all these people treasured was *The Imitation of Christ*, which has been called the second most widely circulated book in Christian history (after the Bible). It continues to be popular today. A recent edition of *Books in Print* lists a dozen different editions of the *Imitation* for sale in the United States—and that counts only English versions.

Attributed to Thomas à Kempis, a fifteenth-century monk in the Netherlands, the *Imitation* was originally written for young monks in formation. Thomas was part of a broad movement in the Low Countries called *Devotio moderna* (present-day piety) that was trying to instill a new sense of holiness in a Catholic population whose religious practice had become lax and tepid. The followers of *Devotio moderna* believed, for instance, that prayer is superior to learning. They rejected the Scholasticism of the day and instead turned to the scriptures and patristic teachings for inspiration. Not knowledge of church doctrine but the simple following of Christ was their ideal.

Thus in Book I of the *Imitation* Thomas declares, "I would rather experience repentance in my soul than know how to define it" (Book I, 1). And, "What good is there in arguing about obscure and recondite matters when ignorance of such things will not be in question on the Day of Judgment?" (Book I, 3).

The *Imitation* insists that the interior disposition of the person is what really matters. In pursuit of this goal Thomas shows a real appreciation for human psychology. He warns constantly about self-deception, about considering oneself as holy, about criticizing others while ignoring one's own faults. Constant vigilance is required. He states, "You will only arrive at a devout inner life by watching over yourself and by being silent with regard to others" (Book II, 5).

The *Imitation of Christ* is divided into four parts, or books, and each of those parts into chapters. Book I offers exhortations useful for spiritual living; Book II contains directions for the inner life, admonishing its readers to be concerned with spiritual rather than materialistic things; Book III takes up consolations of the inner life, often in the form of dialogues with Jesus; Book IV is given entirely to a consideration of the eucharist and how we ought to approach and receive it.

Because *The Imitation of Christ* was aimed at monks, some of its advice (such as turning one's back on the evil world) is more applicable to monastics than laypeople—a fact that has in no way deterred lay readers in the centuries since it was written. Nor have these monastic references barred the *Imitation* from being snatched up by Protestants and members of other religions. Like gold specie, the *Imitation* is accepted everywhere.

In its best translations, *The Imitation of Christ* has an easy, accessible style. This doesn't mean one should read it straight through like a novel or an inspirational essay. The text ought to be taken in little bites, like scripture, by reading, pausing, reflecting, praying. In this way one will find out what people have known for centuries—the *Imitation* is a spiritual classic.

UTOPIA

(1516 ✦ Philosophy)

THOMAS MORE

(1478–1535)

Christian idealists have long yearned to live in a truly just and egalitarian society. Acts 2:44–47 is the earliest expression of this desire. It tells how the first Christians "had all things in common," broke bread together, sold their possessions, and shared the proceeds with the needy. In later centuries, Benedictines and other religious communities strove to live out the same ideal.

Those early Christian experiments in communal living were based on gospel values. By the end of the Middle Ages, however, faith was losing its central place as a basis for social organization. Spurred by the expansion of commerce, people were beginning to ask if rational management could do what religion could not. At least that was the way Thomas More perceived the question.

In 1516 More was negotiating a commercial treaty in Belgium. He was not yet in the service of Henry VIII, who would eventually elevate More to Lord Chancellor of England (and later cut off his head). Given some free time when negotiations stalled, More wrote a treatise on a perfect society maintained by rational consensual agreement.

In it, More claims to meet a traveler named Raphael Hythloday just returned from the island nation of Utopia, located in a distant sea. His visitor describes the Utopian society where all citizens wear identical clothing, live in identical houses, share the work equally, and desire nothing. Leaders are chosen democratically but must not campaign for office. Meals are eaten in common; households are limited to forty persons, and should they exceed that number some of them are moved to other households. Each of the fifty-four cities is laid out in the same manner. It is, in short, a completely planned society.

In the book, More listens to the traveler's account almost without comment, which leaves the reader with mixed feelings. How are we supposed to take this story? Many aspects of Utopia and its ordered life are appealing. Most likely there were features in it that appealed to More as well. His biographer, Peter Ackroyd, observes that More's "own life of discipline, and his devotion to the Catholic Church, suggest that he was naturally inclined to the imposed order of authority . . . [I]t radiated from the centre of More's being."

Yet there is ample evidence that Utopia is not being held up as a perfect society. The name Hythloday means "peddler of nonsense." Utopia itself means "no place." More was a man of high principles that eventually led him to oppose Henry VIII. He could never have lived in Utopia where dissenters are forcibly expatriated.

Above all, Utopia is a land that does not know the law of God. According to Ackroyd, Utopians "have no notion of the origin of humankind and therefore no knowledge of original sin. They have no sense of an imperfect world or of human corruptibility; in that respect, as far as More is concerned, the joke is on them."

When it was first published, *Utopia* was read and debated all over Europe. These days it is most often encountered in political science courses. Yet this short, accessible book continues to offer its seductive dream—or nightmare—and is still worthy of debate.

SPIRITUAL EXERCISES

(c. 1524 ◆ Spirituality)

IGNATIUS LOYOLA

(1491–1556)

Although the *Spiritual Exercises* of Ignatius Loyola is one of the greatest of Catholic spiritual books, it doesn't rate high marks when considered strictly as a reading experience. According to one commentator, "You can read it through, lay it down and wonder, 'What's the big deal?'"

The big deal is its application! To use it profitably one is strongly advised to have a spiritual director experienced with the exercises, or at least to have some kind of spiritual mentoring.

Ignatius began to develop his exercises during the years 1522–23 when he was living near Barcelona and struggling for clarity with his own vocation. His romantic nature tugged at him to make a pilgrimage to Jerusalem. As it turned out, his true mission lay elsewhere. He kept notes on his efforts to reform his life in the expectation that they might be helpful to others. What evolved was a series of meditations designed to bring a person who seriously undertakes the exercises to a deeper and more intentional commitment to Christ.

In their final form, the exercises stretch over four weeks. ("Week" is a flexible term; one "week" may last a few days or might run longer than a calendar week.) The meditations in the first week are aimed at purifying the soul of inordinate attachments. The second week is given to meditations on the life of Jesus so that people can model themselves on Christ. The third week focuses on the passion, coming to see it as the compassionate love of Christ being poured out on the world. The fourth week concentrates on the Risen Lord and is aimed at fostering unselfish love and trust in God.

Unlike his great Spanish contemporaries Teresa of Avila and John of the Cross, Ignatius did not see union with God as the summit point of the exercises. He was an activist. He urged his followers to see how God "conducts himself as one who labors, [creating] the heavens, the elements, plants, fruits, flocks, etc.," then to consider their own calling to engagement. For Ignatius, commitment to Christ is a commitment to the service of others, to the apostolate, and to the church.

Our own time has witnessed a tremendous revival of interest in the *Spiritual Exercises* and in the numbers of people—especially laity—undertaking them. Until fairly recently the exercises were offered in preached retreats, where a director would speak to a roomful of people. Since the 1970s there has been a return to one-on-one directed retreats. Not only are these more intimate and offer greater privacy, but the director is better able to tailor the exercises to individual needs.

Given the experiential nature of the exercises, one may question whether there is any need for them in book form. The answer is yes. Our journey to God is a lifelong process, and while a director is advisable the first time around, with a book one can return to the exercises many times over, with a director or by oneself. In addition, most modern editions of the *Exercises* adapt Ignatius's sometimes archaic language to contemporary ears. So get a copy of your own. The *Spiritual Exercises* have been a great influence for better than four hundred years, and they are not going away any time soon.

A SHORT ACCOUNT OF THE DESTRUCTION OF THE INDIES

(1552 ✦ History)

BARTOLOMÉ DE LAS CASAS

(c. 1474–1566)

A little more than five hundred years ago European adventurers looked for a route to India and stumbled across a new world. Christopher Columbus and the people who followed him were astonished with what they found. On the islands and the mainland there existed flora and fauna unknown in Europe. There were precious metals, jewels, tribal peoples, cities, and developed civilizations. In less than a century, however, the Spanish *conquistadores* had taken much of the land, stolen most of the precious metals, and exterminated most of the population.

How could it happen that Catholic Spain, which undertook exploration in part in order to win souls for the church, carried out mass murder on such a scale? Greed for land and wealth had much to do with it. Among the Spaniards the process was facilitated by the illusion that their victims were not human beings.

Yet not all Spanish believed this. In an Advent sermon in 1511, Antonio Montesinos raised the hackles of the *conquistadores* in Santo Domingo by asking, "Are these [native people] not men? Do they not have rational souls? Are you not obliged to love them as yourselves?" One of the people in church that day was the just-ordained priest Bartolomé de Las Casas from Seville. He began to pay attention to what his countrymen were doing. The more he reflected, the more was he appalled.

Back in Spain, Las Casas wrangled an interview with the aging King Ferdinand and described the atrocities in the Americas. The monarch referred him to the bishop of Burgos who asked, "How does this concern me?" It was a dead end.

So Las Casas threw his energies into a book that might sway public opinion. In haste he drew up an indictment and published it as *A Short Account of the Destruction of the Indies*, describing in graphic detail the horrors suffered by people in Hispaniola, Cuba, Puerto Rico, Central America, Peru, and other places. The book was a publishing success but a political failure. It was read throughout Spain and published in many European languages. However, it failed to change Spanish policies toward native Americans.

Las Casas subsequently became the bishop of Chiapas in southern Mexico. He spent the rest of his life writing, preaching, and stirring up sympathy on behalf of native people.

His *Short Account* is a record of atrocities in the Americas. It recounts how people are speared, hanged, burned alive, thrown to dogs, enslaved, and otherwise brutalized. There were times when the soldiers seemed to make a sport of it. Not even the elderly, children, and pregnant women were spared. They died by the thousands. While the numbers Las Casas claims were killed are suspect, the fundamental facts are not.

The *Short Account* is simply told but not easy to read because of the horrors it describes. It is a crucial book because it speaks truth to power, naming what leaders pretend they don't know.

THE INTERIOR CASTLE

(1577 ✦ Spirituality)

TERESA OF AVILA

(1515–1582)

Prayer is mysterious. Sometimes it is wrapped in words, sometimes not. Other times we find ourselves praying without knowing how it began. So we wonder: Is prayer something we do, or is it something God does in us? What is the shape of prayer? What does it look like and where is it going? Maybe what we really need is a map of the land of prayer.

The Interior Castle of Teresa of Avila is such a map. The great Spanish saint wrote it in 1577 at the suggestion of her confessor. She was sixty-two at the time, worn down by travel and opposition from church authorities who were suspicious of her reform of the Carmelites. A previous book on prayer she had written was being vetted by the Inquisition and was unavailable. She wanted something to give her nuns who, she said, "would better understand the language used between women."

Teresa described the soul at prayer as like a large castle with translucent walls. Inside this castle are seven dwelling places—not rooms exactly, but apartments where one can make a home. Some people remain in the initial dwelling places all their lives; others move on. In the seventh dwells Christ in his glorified humanity whose light illuminates the whole structure.

Teresa takes us room-by-room through this castle, showing us the way into each, the character of the prayer experienced there, and the trials and temptations endemic to each. The first three dwellings are places of prayer that we, ourselves, create. Teresa compares them to a water trough being filled with the help of pipes and aqueducts. The next four dwellings are places of infused prayer that comes from God—like a trough that is constantly replenished by a spring from the center of the earth. Heavenly water, she says, "begins to rise from this spring . . . that is deep within us; it swells and expands our whole interior being, producing ineffable blessings."

Teresa was not an academic. Her advice is wise, practical, and earthy. She wrote this work—one of the greatest treatises on prayer ever produced—in one stroke. Sometimes she gets thrown off the track and apologizes to the reader ("I don't remember what I was talking about, for I have digressed a great deal. . . ."), giving the whole text a feeling of spontaneity. She is a mystic, but she is also someone we would like to know.

The highest state of prayer Teresa describes as a kind of spiritual marriage where the lovers dwell within each other. Teresa is not afraid of sensual metaphors. She urges us to "let the intellect go and surrender oneself into the arms of love, for His Majesty will teach the soul what it must do at that point." Her *Interior Castle* is a wonderful place to visit, an even better place to live.

INTRODUCTION TO
THE DEVOUT LIFE

(1609 ✦ Spirituality)

FRANCIS DE SALES
(1567–1622)

While this notion may seem strange to us today when Rome is so insistent on doctrinal loyalty, the Catholic church in the wake of the Protestant Reformation judged devotion to be more important than doctrine. The three great works of the Counter-Reformation were not catechisms but the *Spiritual Exercises* of Ignatius Loyola, Teresa of Avila's *The Interior Castle*, and the *Introduction to the Devout Life* by Francis de Sales. Of the three, the third was by far the most widely read by rank-and-file Catholics. It offered itself as a manual for Christian living, with practical advice for the devout. For that reason it is very much a product of its era and is probably the most neglected of the three today.

Francis de Sales, born three years after John Calvin died, was appointed Catholic bishop of Geneva, the hotbed of Calvinism, in 1602. He was not a combative type. De Sales descended from Savoy nobility, a learned man, benign in temperament, a skilled communicator. Through his preaching and writing he became a prominent figure in the French church.

Bishop de Sales was also honored for his "care of souls." The art of spiritual guidance was growing in popularity in seventeenth-century Europe. Catholics, especially among the wealthy, were consulting confessors to guide them on the path to perfection and assist them in life decisions. Having been trained in Ignatian spirituality, Francis de Sales was an expert and kindly guide. He was free of Jansenistic rigorism and was ahead of his time in promoting the practice of mental prayer for laypeople.

The *Introduction to the Devout Life*, published in 1609, summarized the kind of spiritual direction de Sales was providing to the noble gentlemen and ladies who flocked to him. The book was an instant success, translated into all the European languages. It was a work of considerable wisdom and piety that told the laity what to do to attain holiness. Alas, the specificity of its direction also dates it for readers today. De Sales, for instance, believed women owed strict obedience to their husbands. He considered whether married couples should have sexual relations on days they receive communion (concluding it was "improper" but not sinful). Dances, he said, are "lawful" but "dangerous." And Catholics should go to confession at least once a week.

The most obvious weakness of the *Introduction* arises from its constituency. Writing for the wealthy nobility, de Sales seems oblivious to the great mass of poor, uneducated Catholics of his day. He even has a chapter titled "How to practice real poverty, being, notwithstanding, really rich." The *Introduction* makes no attempt to link charity with justice or project spirituality into the social order.

In spite of this weakness, the *Introduction to the Devout Life* is a significant work in the history of Christian spirituality. It steered people away from the multiplicity of rote devotions that were still popular in the late Renaissance and anchored holiness firmly in love. True devotion, says Francis de Sales, is nothing less than the love of God. For this reason, *Introduction to the Devout Life* is not only a fascinating window on its age but a work of real wisdom.

THE DARK NIGHT

(1618 ✦ Spirituality)

JOHN OF THE CROSS

(1542–1591)

The prospect of reading John of the Cross unsettles those who have heard something about the Spanish mystic but who never encountered him directly. His name and his *Dark Night* call to mind the tortured journey to God by a mystical elite who suffer painful aridity, near despair, and perhaps emotional depression in the process. It sure doesn't sound like fun.

This popular view of John of the Cross does not do him justice. To be sure, the Carmelite poet and mystic does write for those who seek after God seriously, rather than those who just "say their prayers." And it is true he believed that of the great mass of believers only a few take the plunge and achieve a deep mystical union with God. Yet there is no reason to doubt some degree of mysticism is within the range of most believers. God's invitation is always there. And those who do take the plunge will find in John of the Cross a sane and down-to-earth mentor.

The Dark Night (the author never called it *Dark Night of the Soul*) describes the journey of a soul from self-centeredness to eventual union with God. The entire process is first recounted symbolically in a poem of eight stanzas reminiscent of the *Song of Songs*. In the poem, after traversing a dark landscape and climbing a mystical ladder, the soul finds its lover and is joined with him in a sensual, almost erotic, way:

"I lost myself. Forgot myself.
I lay my face against the Beloved's face.
Everything fell away and I left myself behind. . . ."

The rest of the book is a commentary on the poem. The book is divided into two sections describing what John calls the Night of the Sense and the Night of the Spirit.

The Night of the Sense comprises that period when a beginner in the spiritual life is first granted consolations and then finds them taken away—a process that is painful and distressing to the person involved. John of the Cross compares it to a child who has enjoyed his mother's breast and soft foods but who is finally weaned and set on his own two feet to partake of the "crusty bread" of adulthood. During this stage the beginner is purified of sinful habits. John comments on each of the seven deadly sins as they apply to spiritual progress. This process can't be rushed; the beginner has to endure it patiently.

Once that phase is over, the seeker (now an "adept") enters into the Night of the Spirit, which, if anything, is darker and deeper than the previous phase. Now the soul learns to depend on God alone. It is more painful only because the soul's yearning for God is more intense. In reality God is infusing the soul with light, but the soul can't see it yet; it believes itself in darkness even as God's fire is purifying it, until at last it has nothing but God. "Only then," says John, "radically empty, stripped naked of the old self, is [the soul] truly poor in spirit. Only then can she live that new and blessed life. This is the dark night. This is what yields union with God."

Reading John of the Cross is not a depressing experience. His *Dark Night* is essential reading for anyone who seriously seeks the light.

PENSÉES

(1669 ✦ Apologetics)

BLAISE PASCAL
(1623–1662)

It happened on the night of November 23, 1654—a religious experience that changed his life. Blaise Pascal could scarcely find words to describe it. It went on for about two hours, from half past ten to half past midnight. Afterward, he wrote, "FIRE. God of Abraham, God of Isaac, God of Jacob, not of philosophers and scholars. Certainty, certainty, heartfelt, joy, peace. God of Jesus Christ . . . Joy, joy, joy, tears of Joy . . ." It was such an overwhelming moment for him that Pascal had his account transcribed onto parchment and sewn into his coat. He carried it with him for the rest of his life.

At the time Pascal was already world-famous as a mathematician and scientist. He had invented the barometer and the adding machine, and advanced the understanding of geometry and scientific methodology. Until 1654 he had been a devout but nominal Catholic, but after his "night of fire" he threw himself into religious projects, including the writing of his *Pensées* (Thoughts), which were published after his death at the age of thirty-nine.

What were these thoughts? Pascal envisioned a defense of Christianity—an apologetic—that would appeal to lukewarm Christians or skeptics. The Enlightenment was threatening to undermine traditional religion, replacing faith with reason. In the *Pensées*, Pascal argues that faith is reasonable and is consistent with the ordered world that scientists encounter at every hand. In his famous wager that appears in the book, he even proposes that believing in God is the most sensible option for people: believing makes one happy in the short and long term, while the denial of God—if one bets against God's existence—can result in eternal damnation.

In writing these *Pensées* Pascal championed the views of the Jansenists, a splinter group of intellectuals to which Pascal and his family were ardently attached. Jansenists (named after Bishop Cornelius Jansen of Ypres) took a bleak view of humankind, declaring that humans are so fatally scarred by sin they cannot attain salvation themselves and so must throw themselves on God's grace. Passionate in their devotions, puritanical in their morals, the Jansenists believed that life was hard, salvation difficult, and that only a select few would see God in heaven.

Pascal is held in the highest esteem in France for the purity and beauty of his language, especially in his *Pensées* and *Provincial Letters*. Alas, this quality is lost on readers who encounter him in translation. In addition, the *Pensées* were never completed in the author's lifetime. What we have are fragmentary notes for a book, sometimes several paragraphs in a row, sometimes just a sentence or phrase. Pascal had an outline for the whole, but there are disagreements among scholars about how the fragments fit together. It is impossible to read the *Pensées* as one would read an ordinary book.

Still, what strikes the reader today is the fervid quality of the work. Here is a writer who believes these are issues of life and death. He urges us: Take the plunge. Trust your instincts. Follow your heart. Don't try to reason it out, because rationality is flawed. "The heart has its reasons that reason does not know." Pascal wants us, his readers, to open ourselves to God's fire and "certainty, certainty, heartfelt, joy, peace . . ."

THE PRACTICE OF THE
PRESENCE OF GOD

(1693 ◆ Spirituality)

LAWRENCE OF THE RESURRECTION
(1611–1691)

From the little we know of him, he was born Nicholas Herman to a poor family in the Lorraine region of France. As a young man he served in the Thirty Years War, was taken prisoner once and later wounded fighting the Swedes. He took a position as a footman to a Parisian banker but lost it for being a clumsy oaf. At loose ends, he became a Carmelite lay brother like his uncle, taking the name Lawrence of the Resurrection. At the Paris Carmel he was put into the kitchen and stayed there for thirty years. If you saw him, you would not think much of him: a large, ungraceful man who walked with a limp, doing menial work.

Those who looked more closely, however, discerned that his soul was airy and bright. After a time, more people noticed and asked him why he was so happy. He said he just tried to love God in everything he did. He lived in God's presence, speaking his love for God over and over. They asked him, aren't you afraid you are deceiving yourself? Brother Lawrence answered that, if so, God would take care of it.

People started coming to him for guidance or wrote him letters seeking advice. Brother Lawrence answered them all in a simple, straightforward way. Because his leg bothered him he was eventually put in the cobbler's room where he could sit and make sandals for the community. Abbé de Beaufort, vicar-general to the archbishop of Paris, met him there for conversations and took notes on Brother Lawrence's words. Eventually, it is said, all of

Paris knew about Brother Lawrence. François Fénelon, the famous preacher, visited him and came away impressed.

At the age of eighty, Brother Lawrence of the Resurrection died. Abbé de Beaufort looked at his notes once more, put them together with some letters Brother Lawrence had written, and published them in a little book called *The Practice of the Presence of God*. Readers devoured it; they read it then and have read it ever since—clergy and laypeople, Catholics, Protestants, Anglicans, Orthodox, and others, in almost every language in which books are published.

Brother Lawrence didn't teach a prayer method. He taught a way of life that was simple, positive, and heartfelt. He placed himself in God's presence and remained there, speaking words of love. As he did, he felt himself drawn more deeply and tenderly into God's presence. "My most usual method is simple attentiveness and a loving gaze upon God, to whom I often feel united with more happiness and gratification than a baby at its mother's breast. . . . Indeed . . . I would willingly call this state 'the breasts of God.'"

Brother Lawrence made it absolutely clear that his way took effort, especially at first. On the other hand, it is not complicated. The only requirements are desire, a loving heart, and trust that God will make everything happen.

The Practice of the Presence of God can be read in an hour's time. It can nourish a person a lifetime.

ABANDONMENT TO DIVINE PROVIDENCE

(1861 ✦ Spirituality)

JEAN-PIERRE DE CAUSSADE
(1675–1751)

When it comes to soul nourishment, sometimes the simplest wisdom is the most illuminating, and the plainest words the most memorable. Jean-Pierre de Caussade, an eighteenth-century Jesuit, had two pieces of advice that he repeated over and over: Give yourself wholly to God, and be alive to every moment. These have resonated so deeply with people that his writing is still treasured, even though it had to wait a hundred years after he died to be published.

Caussade was for several years the spiritual director for the nuns of the Visitation convent at Nancy, France. The sisters so valued his insights that they saved his retreat talks and his letters written while traveling. After Caussade died the sisters were tempted to publish them but decided not to, because the church in those days was suspicious of quietism (the heretical belief that a soul can be so absorbed in God that it does not need a church or sacraments, etc.). It wasn't until 1861 that the talks and letters were edited by another Jesuit and published in a book that ensured Caussade's reputation.

As a Jesuit, Caussade was used to being moved around by his superiors—now a pastor, now a chaplain, now a teacher. He didn't always like the assignments, but he learned to accept them. Reflecting on this, he concluded that what was good for Jesuits was good for people generally: Accept what comes to you—the situation you find yourself in is the very place you will encounter Christ and find salvation. And as a natural result: Live wholly in the moment you find yourself in, not in the past that cannot be changed or the future you cannot control. Caussade calls it "the sacrament of the moment."

Abandonment to Divine Providence proclaims that holiness is basically easy—it is just a matter of doing ordinary things with all of our heart. "Consider your life," writes Caussade, "and you will see that it consists of countless trifling actions. Yet God is quite satisfied with them." According to Caussade, sanctity requires

> "only that we accept what we often cannot avoid, and endure with love and resignation things which could cause us weariness and disgust . . . This is what being holy means. It is the mustard seed which is almost too small to be recognized or harvested, the drachma of the Gospels, the treasure that no one finds, as it is thought to be too well hidden to be looked for."

Once we see the everydayness of life as God's invitation, then it follows that "the present moment is always overflowing with immeasurable riches, far more than [we] are able to hold." Each moment is like a fountain of living water. We should accept it and be filled—not seeking elsewhere for grace when it is as near to us as our breath.

There is a thread of anti-intellectualism running through Caussade, as there was with Thomas à Kempis. Reading and theological speculation are often put aside when people believe the Holy Spirit is whispering in their ear. Yet there is wisdom here, too. *Abandonment to Divine Providence* explores a powerfully incarnational theme that later surfaced in the "little way" of Thérèse of Lisieux. And it can still nourish us. This very moment.

APOLOGIA PRO VITA SUA

(1865 ✦ Autobiography)

JOHN HENRY NEWMAN
(1801–1890)

Rarely has a controversy between two men resulted in a great work of literature, but in the 1860s just that thing happened. The two men were Charles Kingsley and John Henry Newman. Kingsley was an Anglican divine and professor of history at Cambridge University. He had a reputation as a champion of the working poor, popularizing his socialist ideas in a series of novels, most of them forgotten today. His best-known work is a children's book, *Water Babies*, still read in the twenty-first century.

Kingsley had other axes to grind besides socialism. Like many educated Englishmen of his day he harbored deep anti-Semitic and anti-Catholic prejudices. In a book review he accused the Catholic church of deliberate dishonesty—indeed, of having made dishonesty a pastoral practice. And one of the foremost practitioners of that art, said Kingsley, was John Henry Newman.

Newman at the time was living quietly in an oratory near Birmingham. Although he stayed out of public view, he was, if anything, even better known than Kingsley. Newman had been the foremost Anglican clergyman in England, an essayist, poet, preacher, and fellow of Oriel College at Oxford, who in 1845 abruptly renounced the Anglican communion and joined the Catholic church. He was ordained a priest in Rome and returned to England, respected by many, but considered a traitor by many others.

Newman's scholarly but combative nature was galvanized by Kingsley's allegation that "truth . . . ha[s] never been a virtue with the Roman clergy. Father Newman informs us that it need not, and on the whole ought not to be. . . ." There followed an exchange of letters in the press. When Kingsley followed with a pamphlet attacking him, Newman saw the need to compose something more substantial in reply. In the months from April to June 1864 he wrote a masterpiece. *Apologia pro Vita Sua* was snatched up by periodicals, where it was serialized, and devoured by an admiring public that was both impressed and entertained. Using wit and scholarship, Newman demolished the pretensions of Kingsley and his followers. Yet, while presenting his arguments in a way to win debating points, Newman realized he needed to open his heart to curious readers, many of whom were still suspicious of his motives for becoming Catholic. In this regard *Apologia pro Vita Sua* transcends mere controversy. Newman reveals himself as a man who is generous to friends, earnest in his intellectual struggle, and frank about his own pains and self-doubts. The book also earned him a place as the greatest prose stylist of his day. Even people who were not coreligionists memorized portions of the *Apologia*, so perfectly expressed were its sentiments and reasoning.

To readers a century and a half later, *Apologia pro Vita Sua* may seem excessively formal and stiff. Some readers find its vocabulary too rich; its sentences are long and adorned with numerous interjections and subordinate clauses, replete with references to people long dead. However one cannot read Newman as one would read a bestseller today. He was raised in an era that prized intellectual discourse, and the structure of his prose reflects a beautiful balance of reason and inquiry. A written sentence of Newman is like a yacht cutting through the water. One must take it in slowly, savor its lines and symmetry, and acknowledge its truth and compelling destination. In the process, one encounters a great man and a great soul.

RERUM NOVARUM

(1891 ✦ Documentation)

POPE LEO XIII
(1810–1903)

For centuries the West was synonymous with "Christendom." It was Christendom that shaped the Middle Ages, that confronted expansionist Islam, and that discovered the New World. The Protestant Reformation modified Christendom, but didn't diminish it. More than just an identifiable population, Christendom was a transnational oligarchy made up of royalty, the aristocracy, and the church. It was a ruling consortium of privilege and power.

By the middle of the nineteenth century, however, historic Christendom was in tatters. The French Revolution in the late eighteenth century and popular uprisings in the nineteenth overthrew many hereditary monarchies. The Roman church was shorn of its territories and the pope was made a virtual prisoner in the Vatican. Finally, aristocratic families were replaced by a new elite—bourgeois capitalists created by the Industrial Revolution. Pope Pius IX tried to pump life into the old alliance in 1864 when he issued his *Syllabus of Errors* that condemned "progress, liberalism, and modern civilization." The church Pius ruled shuddered at the specter of socialism inciting the masses. In another document Pius urged industrial workers to be content with their lot, since "the Catholic Church teaches . . . slaves to remain true to their masters."

By 1891, however, there was a new pope in Rome and a new agenda for the church. Pope Leo XIII was born to an aristocratic Roman family but had come to realize it was time for the church to end its ancient alliance with the monied class and instead cast its lot with the workers. In the encyclical *Rerum Novarum* (On New Things), Leo spoke bluntly of a world where "a small number of very rich men have been able to lay upon the teeming masses of the laboring poor a yoke little better than that of slavery itself."

What was his agenda for change? While it surely wasn't socialism, Leo was not beyond adopting the tactics of socialists. He endorsed the right of workers to form unions and, when absolutely necessary, to strike for better wages and working conditions. He warned about placing young children in factories, and he called upon governments to support the rights of workers because "the State has for its office to protect natural rights, not to destroy them."

Rerum Novarum is more like a document than a book, yet this document was a watershed moment for the Catholic church. Written in officialese, cautious in many respects, the encyclical nevertheless was a fateful break with the politics of old. It abandoned the carcass of Christendom and turned the church's face to the plight of the masses and the poor. In years to come the policy would support the rise of Christian Democratic parties in many European nations, produce further encyclicals in support of labor (e.g., Pope Pius XI's *Quadragisimo Anno* in 1931), and pave the way for a broader "option for the poor" by the church toward the end of the millennium. To the discerning reader, *Rerum Novarum*, even with all its bureaucratic prose, reads like a trumpet blast.

STORY OF A SOUL

(1899 ♦ Autobiography)

THÉRÈSE OF LISIEUX

(1873–1897)

When Thérèse Martin died of tuberculosis at the age of twenty-four in 1897, there were sisters in her convent who predicted she would soon be forgotten. What is there to remember about someone so young? They didn't realize that Thérèse's sister Pauline, prioress of the Carmelite convent, had asked the younger woman to write a brief account of her life. After Thérèse died, Pauline changed the parts she didn't like, printed two thousand copies of her edited version, and sent them to Carmelite houses around France. Within months those two thousand copies had been multiplied many times over. In two years time the Martin family was forced to move out of Lisieux by the hordes of visitors who wanted to see where Thérèse had grown up.

What is it about *Story of a Soul* that so fascinated people then and now? First, there is the transparent holiness of the writer. Thérèse of Lisieux wrote directly and without artifice. She was a writer of total sincerity. Second, the path to holiness she described and lived is simplicity itself. Thérèse called it her "little way." She undertook no heroic acts, only small, hidden things that could be done without people noticing. They were small things, yet they were prompted by burning, passionate love for God and suffering humanity.

Thérèse was the ninth and last child born to devout Catholic parents in Alençon, in Normandy. Later the family moved to Lisieux, near Caen. Four siblings died in infancy, leaving five sisters, four of whom eventually entered the Carmelite cloister.

Coddled and caressed in her family, Thérèse felt herself likewise coddled and caressed by God with whom she built a relationship of unshakable trust. She referred to herself as God's "little flower," his "little bird" who was nevertheless drawn into God's "fiery furnace" of love. Her confidence in God made her absolutely fearless, so that she could announce, " . . . *Love* has chosen me as a holocaust, me, a weak and imperfect creature. Is not this choice worthy of *Love?* Yes, in order that Love be fully satisfied, it is necessary that It lower Itself, and that It lower itself to nothingness and transform this nothingness into *fire*."

The first readers of *Story of a Soul* had only Pauline's edited version and were sometimes put off by Thérèse's sentimental style. In 1972, however, a new critical edition recaptured the original text and added other writings that offered a fuller picture of the young saint. No longer just the sweet teenager, this new Thérèse revealed herself as a powerful woman who aspired to be a warrior, a priest, an apostle, and a martyr. Although a cloistered nun, her imagination extended far beyond its walls to embrace a suffering world. She was not content with a safe place in heaven, but proclaimed, "I will return! I will come down! I want to spend my heaven doing good on earth."

HEART OF DARKNESS

(1902 ◆ Fiction)

JOSEPH CONRAD

(1857–1924)

Oscar Wilde once observed that sin is an essential element of progress. Joseph Conrad surely shared that cynical view. The son of a Polish aristocrat who became a steamship captain and then one of England's greatest novelists, Conrad wrote about people who set out to civilize foreign lands but who were co-opted and broken by the dark forces they unleashed. The nineteenth and early twentieth centuries marked the high tide of colonialism in Africa, Asia, and South America. Conrad had seen those places in his years of travel. What did he find? Rapacious exploitation. Wrongheaded idealism. Sin.

Heart of Darkness, one of his greatest stories, is narrated by a fictional character named Marlow, who serves as a sensitive but impartial observer of the action. Sitting with his friends aboard a ship in the peaceful Thames River, Marlow relates how he was hired by a firm to command a steamer on an African river, visiting the firm's many colonial outposts. From the beginning one gathers from Marlow's account the waste and moral decay of the whole enterprise. European machinery sits rusting in the weeds. A French gunboat is seen in the distance, impotently shelling a jungle shore. Native people are enslaved and used as throwaway resources. Marlow is appalled.

He is assured that there is one agent, far up the river, who has successfully collected large amounts of ivory. The agent's name is Kurtz, "a very remarkable person" who "will be a somebody in the Administration before long." Another describes Kurtz as "an emissary of pity, and science, and progress, and the devil knows what else."

So Marlow begins his long ascent up the river, a journey into darkest Africa, which is also an ascent into the darkness of the heart of colonialism. The trip is filled with adventure and mounting fear. When the ailing Kurtz is finally located, it becomes clear that local people have made him into a god—an honor which Kurtz accepts as his due. But he has become a god of death, not of life. As the steamer heads down the river once more with the dying man, he comes to recognize his own dark delusions, leaving him empty and despairing.

Heart of Darkness has been taken as a parable for our century of exploitation. Francis Ford Coppola transplanted it to Southeast Asia during the Vietnam War in his bleak 1979 film *Apocalypse Now*.

The saddest part of all, according to Joseph Conrad, is that "civilized" people, including Kurtz's fiancée back in Europe, cannot face the reality of what they have loosed on the world. They prefer to live in illusion, believing that imposed "progress" is good for everyone and that agents of progress are heroes.

Conrad's story makes it clear that Africa is not the only corrupted place. In the end, even the tranquil Thames where Marlow and his party sit "seemed to lead into the heart of an immense darkness."

ORTHODOXY

(1908 ♦ Apologetics)

G. K. CHESTERTON

(1874–1936)

If a man is not to believe in himself, in what is he to believe?" This question was once asked of Gilbert Keith Chesterton, prompting the British man of letters to go home and write a book on the subject—the book that became *Orthodoxy*. It was a predictable outcome, since, as Chesterton joked, he was "only too ready to write books upon the feeblest provocation." But the book in this case became a classic of Christian apologetics, influencing generations of people who struggled with belief, including such men and women as C. S. Lewis, E. F. Schumacher, and Dorothy Day.

G. K. Chesterton (as he was commonly known) was a work unto himself. Although he never graduated from a university, he became a journalist, biographer, novelist (his Father Brown mysteries are still read), an economist of sorts, humorist, poet, debater, public speaker, and excelled at them all. He was an enormous man—somewhere over three hundred pounds. When an elderly woman scolded him during World War I by asking, "Why aren't you out at the front?" Chesterton replied, "My dear madam, if you will step around this way a little, you will see that I *am*."

For all his calculated clowning, Chesterton had a streak of melancholy that gave depth to his person and his writing. In his twenties he went through a breakdown that was both emotional and spiritual. His marriage in 1901 contributed to his healing, as did his renunciation of skepticism and return to the Anglican church. He later became a Roman Catholic.

Orthodoxy dates from his Anglican years. It is not, as one might suppose, a defense of Christian doctrine as such but an attack on the illusions of progress and an argument for the return to eternal verities. Progress, says Chesterton, is not achieved by changing the vision. It is achieved by changing the world to conform to the vision. And this vision, he says, was fixed in place "before the foundations of the world." Harking back to the original question, he thought that believing in oneself was a sorry substitute for believing in God.

In *Orthodoxy* Chesterton delights in exposing the confused thinking of his philosophical opponents. He skewers them with paradox, his trademark literary device, and he is endlessly quotable. "There are some desires that are not desirable," he remarks at one point. And later: "It is easy to be a madman; it is easy to be a heretic. It is always easy to let the age have its head; the difficult thing is to keep one's own."

G. K. Chesterton was a conservative by temperament and conviction, but his conservatism has a Jeffersonian flavor. He believed in small communities of people living simply, faithful to the "original good." He was suspicious of philosophical fads such as "pantheism, evolutionism, and modern cosmic religion." He was a gentleman who believed that argument and human discourse—mixed with laughter—could change attitudes. His agrarian conservatism can be refreshing, especially compared to the imperial conservatism that dominates religious discourse in our day. While some of the evils he jousted with may not be familiar to contemporary readers, his evocation of primal faith—"mere Christianity," as C. S. Lewis called it—still rings true a hundred years later.

THE MONTESSORI METHOD

(1909 ✦ Education)

MARIA MONTESSORI

(1870–1952)

Maria Montessori was a pioneer in more ways than one. The daughter of wealthy middle-class parents, she elected to study medicine in Rome and in 1896 became the first woman to earn an M.D. from the University of Rome. Her medical colleagues didn't quite know what to do with her and so shunted her off to the pediatric ward of a mental hospital—which was fine with her.

Her study of Down syndrome children (then referred to as "idiot children") convinced her that many of them could learn. The educational program she devised produced astonishing results. Some of her children tested at the same level as public school students. Dr. Montessori next took her system to young children of the slums and created her first *casa dei bambini* in a housing project. Again, she produced stellar results. Educators from around the world began to pay attention. In 1909 she published *The Montessori Method* that explained the theory and practice behind her schools.

The Montessori method is based essentially on freedom. Instead of passively sitting at bolted-down desks and chairs, her students share long tables with classmates and are encouraged to get up and move around. Dr. Montessori believed that liberty requires activity. She wanted her charges to explore their environment and devise solutions to situations they encountered there. It was the teacher's role, she said, to be passive, to observe, intervening only when necessary.

Maria Montessori's ideas were borrowed in part from French educators, but she was the first to put them systematically to use in classrooms. She depended heavily on her own incarnational instincts that grew out of her religious faith. A devout Catholic, she often quoted the scriptures in support of her theories. She was convinced that children aged three to five had "adult souls" that needed to be called forth.

There are probably other books more useful than this one for describing the nuts and bolts of Montessori-style schooling for teachers today. *The Montessori Method* is of interest chiefly as a historical document that explains how the method first came to be used. The author acknowledges that this book represents "incomplete notes." While much of it is dated, it is dated in the way any foundational document is dated: locked into its time but fascinating for the light it casts on the present.

Despite the author's hopes, *The Montessori Method* failed to revolutionize educational theory after it was published. In the United States it had to struggle against theories of John Dewey. Montessori's system was geared to individual creativity; Dewey's stressed socialization and was judged to be a better "fit" for the twentieth-century American ethos.

Still, Montessori schools live on. Today the American Montessori Society in New York claims more than 10,000 individual members. In 2005 there were about 5,000 Montessori schools of all kinds in the United States.

Toward the end of her life, Dr. Montessori ran afoul of Benito Mussolini and was exiled to India, then moved to the Netherlands. But Italy never forgot her. Right up until the Euro came into circulation, Maria Montessori's image graced the 1,000 lira note, usurping the place once held by Marco Polo.

THE TRAGIC SENSE OF LIFE

(1913 ✦ Philosophy)

MIGUEL DE UNAMUNO

(1864–1936)

Miguel de Unamuno once wrote a novel about a priest who lost his religious conviction. Out of compassion for his flock, however, he carried on his ministry as usual and didn't tell anyone. In some ways the story could be about Unamuno himself: He was a man who struggled with faith, questioning many tenets of belief, yet who insisted on the need for a spiritual basis in life. The work for which he is best known is a volume of "poetic philosophy" titled *The Tragic Sense of Life*, published in Spain in 1913 and in English nearly a decade later.

What is the tragedy Unamuno writes about? It is death, or, more precisely, the desire for immortality when confronted with personal annihilation. A thoroughly modern man, Unamuno claims he can no longer swallow the old arguments for God's existence. They are rationalistic, and he scorned rationalism. "Against values of the heart," he says, "reasons do not avail. For reasons are only reasons—that is to say, they are not even truths." Nor are assurances from the church any longer sufficient. Unamuno, a scholar of Greek literature, was well aware of the myths that underlay Christian narratives. Myths he appreciated, but not when they were packaged as facts.

Death, on the other hand, is an inevitable fact. How can the individual find a way around it? For Unamuno the answer lies with desire and with passion. The depth of our desire for immortality must signal something, he declares. Where did it come from? It must be planted in our being. It must be true because we *feel* it, claims Unamuno, arguing from the particular to the universal. Elsewhere he argues that we are not moral because we believe in God; we believe in God because we are moral and find goodness within ourselves.

Unamuno's *Tragic Sense of Life* is not a formal work of philosophy. He was a classicist—a professor of Greek and rector of Salamanca University as well as Spain's best-known writer in the period between the world wars. He was proud of his Spanish heritage, but he did not represent the refined, delicate tradition of Seville or even Madrid. Unamuno was a Basque, a passionate and muscular writer. His prose leans heavily on the imperative. Exclamation points abound. In one place he announces, ". . . he above all deserves immortality who desires it passionately, even in the face of reason."

Unamuno knew this sounded absurd. He didn't shrink from absurdity but relished it. For him, faith always bordered on the absurd anyway, especially coming to God out of our great longing:

"To believe in God is to long for his existence and, further, it is to act as if he existed; it is to live by this longing and to make it the inner spring of our action. This longing or hunger for divinity begets hope, hope begets faith, and faith and hope beget charity. Of this divine longing is born our sense of beauty, of finality, of goodness."

The Tragic Sense of Life ends with a tribute to Spain, which stands on the fringe of Europe but which, for that reason, is better able to translate the East to the West. Spain, Unamuno says, is like Don Quixote who was judged by everyone to be a fool and doomed to fail in all his adventures. Yet Quixote was a tragic hero too; he retained his idealism and compassion even in defeat, even when it was most absurd.

POEMS

(1918 ✦ Poetry)

GERARD MANLEY HOPKINS

(1844–1889)

Are these poems or prayers? Because they deal almost exclusively with spiritual themes and are reprinted in prayer books, including the appendix of the *Liturgy of the Hours*, one might conclude that Gerard Manley Hopkins was a writer of pious verse. Of his piety there is no question—he was a convert to Catholicism and a priest. Yet Hopkins was much more than a versifier. He was a major poet of the Victorian era, an original voice, an experimenter with poetic forms, and for all of the light that shone in his poems there was more than a little darkness. Consider his poem "Spring and Fall: to a young child":

> Márgarét, áre you gríeving
> Over Goldengrove unleaving?
> Leáves líke the things of man, you
> With your fresh thoughts care for, can you?
> Áh! ás the heart grows older
> It will come to such sights colder
> By and by, nor spare a sigh
> Though worlds of wanwood leafmeal lie;
> And yet you will weep and know why.
> Now no matter, child, the name:
> Sórrow's spríngs áre the same.
> Nor mouth had, no nor mind, expressed
> What heart heard of, ghost guessed:

It is the blight that man was born for,
It is Margaret your mourn for.

"Spring and Fall" captures the inevitable sadness and grief that often surface in Hopkins's poetry, but it also exhibits the word-play, the rhythm, and elegant music of his writing.

Hopkins was a product of the Oxford Movement that aimed to reform the Anglican church and that brought many Anglicans into the Roman church in mid-nineteenth-century England. It was a bumpy transition to make. The young Hopkins wrote to John Henry Newman, "I . . . have heard [from] my father and mother in return for my letter announcing my conversion. Their answers are terrible: I cannot read them twice." While he was fulfilled in his new faith, Hopkins never quite fit in. "His mind runs in eccentric ways," said a Jesuit superior. The convert-priest was also prone to depression.

Hopkins had written poetry early in life but burned all his poems when he entered the Society of Jesus. Later he returned to writing. His poems were published only after his death, thanks to British poet laureate Robert Bridges.

The poetry of Gerard Manley Hopkins expresses the joy of faith intertwined with the struggle of faith. Some of his poems, such as "Carrion Comfort," are very dark indeed. But this is precisely what makes his poetry readable today and him more than a sentimental Victorian. Nurtured by the *Spiritual Exercises* of Ignatius Loyola, Hopkins believed firmly that even "blue-bleak embers" could flash out in divine fire and that darkness was not our permanent condition,

Because the Holy Ghost over the bent
World broods with warm breast and with ah! bright wings.

KRISTIN LAVRANSDATTER

(1922 ✦ Fiction)

SIGRID UNDSET

(1882–1949)

Sigrid Undset was baptized in the Lutheran church in her native Norway but drifted away from it by the time she was due to be confirmed. She came back to Christianity after achieving success as a novelist, but this time as a Catholic.

There was a belief in nineteenth-century Scandinavia that the Catholic church had never been deeply rooted there. Medieval Catholicism, it was claimed, had failed to capture the imagination of the population. Undset, the daughter of a noted archaeologist, sided with those who believed Catholicism in the Middle Ages was woven deeply into the fabric of Norwegian life, and she wrote *Kristin Lavransdatter* partly as a way of supporting her conviction.

Kristin Lavransdatter is a trilogy of novels set in Norway in the first half of the fourteenth century. In *The Wreath*, Kristin rebels against the marriage her father arranged and instead falls in love with the charming but thoughtless Erland Nikolausson. Not only do they violate kinship bonds with Kristin's father, but they indirectly cause the death of Erland's mistress. In *The Wife*, Kristin and Erland, now married, make their home in a remote area of central Norway where they live uneasily with the local population. Kristin bears Erland seven sons, but the marriage is difficult for them both. They have the first of their many separations. The third novel, *The Cross*, spans many years. Kristin manages Erland's estate and watches over their sons. Erland is killed defending her from malicious gossip. Finally, the boys having grown, Kristin enters a convent just as the Black Death reaches Norway's shores.

Unlike other novels written around the same time, Undset's are remarkable for not romanticizing the Middle Ages. She captures the daily life of people in vivid detail—customs, living arrangements, travel, politics, labor, and religious practice. In her telling, the family and the church were the twin centers of life for fourteenth-century people. The medieval ideal of courtly love still had its hold on people—which doesn't mean they repressed eroticism. In fact, Undset's handling of intimate love scenes upset some readers when the novels first appeared in the 1920s.

Undset's familiarity with Norse sagas and folklore influenced the form and language of her books. She developed a practice of limiting her vocabulary to Old Norse words and utilizing the syntax and sentence arrangement of the sagas—which mostly followed an oral tradition. It gives her writing a unique narrative flow.

Kristin Lavransdatter earned Undset the Nobel Prize for Literature in 1928. The work has been neglected in English-speaking countries, in part because the original translation by Charles Archer tried to achieve a medieval idiom by using archaic words and phrasing. Readers found it a hard slog. The award-winning translation by Tiina Nunnally, completed in 2000, eliminated the fussy Victorian tone and is more faithful to Undset's original text. There is reason to hope it will win new readers for this classic work.

THE SPIRIT OF CATHOLICISM

(1924 ◆ Theology)

KARL ADAM

(1876–1966)

Karl Adam is probably the most influential of the twentieth-century theologians who worked in the era just before the Second Vatican Council (Vatican II). His *Spirit of Catholicism*, published in Germany in 1924 and in English five years later, made him world famous. Through his writing and from his chair of theology at Tübingen he had a profound effect on popular readers as well as on a generation of theologians and church leaders.

Adam was a Bavarian who did his early work in moral theology. He was well-versed in patristics, and was one of the thinkers of his day who edged Catholic theology away from Scholasticism to a firmer anchor in scripture. It was Adam who used the Pauline image of vine and branches to popularize the church as the Mystical Body of Christ.

The Spirit of Catholicism was written in part to combat the subjectivity of Emmanuel Kant still popular in the 1920s. Adam implored his readers to escape "the hermitage of self" and see the church as something more coherent than a "haphazard collection of individuals." In place of that notion he proposed a scriptural model of the church as an organism whose members stand in purposeful relation to each other. He wrote, ". . . the church possesses the Spirit of Christ, not as a collection of single individuals, nor as a sum of spiritual personalities, but as a compact, ordered unity of the faithful, as a community that transcends the individual . . . and expresses itself in a sacred hierarchy. . . ."

Karl Adam's model was a considerable advance over the ecclesiology of the day and bore fruit in the encyclicals *Mystici Corporis* (1943) of Pius XII and *Ecclesiam Suam* (1964) of Paul VI. Little wonder Rome endorsed him, since Adam had an exalted view of the office of pope. He wrote, "The original nature of the Church, her fundamental determination as a unitary organism, achieves its purest expression in the papacy." He could rhapsodize over a pontifical high mass and maintained that when a believer kisses the pope's hand "he kisses all his brethren, who are joined together into one in the person of the pope."

Adam's picture of the church is appealing because it is a romantic one, strongly colored by his own romantic nature. As a theologian this was his strength and his weakness. When National Socialism was on the rise, Adam was an early supporter. He defended the racial legislation of the Nazis and as late as 1943 published a theological essay that reeked of anti-Semitism. At the same time Adam was aware of Nazism's neo-pagan leanings and spoke publicly against them—to the point where his residence was machine-gunned by Nazi hooligans, forcing him to find lodging with his bishop.

But that occurred two decades after publication of *The Spirit of Catholicism*, which, by mid-century, was considered the finest single summary of the Catholic ethos. Vatican II would change that view. Karl Adam, however, was one of the figures who made Vatican II possible.

BLACK ELK SPEAKS

(1932 ✦ Biography)

JOHN G. NEIHARDT

(1881–1973)

In August of 1930 John Neihardt, a poet raised in Missouri, was collecting oral histories from Native Americans as background for his writing about the frontier. He heard that a Lakota medicine man named Black Elk had stories to tell, so Neihardt went to the Pine Ridge Reservation in South Dakota to meet him.

Thus began one of the great collaborations in American letters. Black Elk had been at some of the climactic events of the struggle by Native Americans against European intruders. He had been at Little Big Horn in 1876 when Custer was defeated and at Wounded Knee in 1890 when the Sioux were massacred in retaliation. He was a cousin of Crazy Horse, the great Sioux leader. He had been a member of Buffalo Bill's Wild West Show, traveling with it to Europe to perform before Queen Victoria.

More than merely witnessing historical events, however, Black Elk was a living repository of Native American ethnography. As a medicine man, he was intimately acquainted with Lakota spiritual traditions—its dances and pipe ceremonies—which by 1930 were mostly forgotten by the younger Sioux. The book Neihardt eventually wrote preserved these traditions and turned Black Elk into a cult figure.

Why *Black Elk Speaks* is included in a collection of Catholic books is another story. Nicholas Black Elk (to use his baptismal name) became a Christian convert and eventually a catechist for the Catholic church, bringing many Sioux to Catholicism (for more details, see *Black Elk's Religion: The Sun Dance and Lakota Catholicism* by Clyde Holler).

Black Elk Speaks records the memories of a Christian looking back to his non-Christian days. When it first appeared in 1932, Black Elk's Jesuit mentors were appalled, since he spoke of his Native American religion with great reverence. Perhaps fortunately for him at that time, the book was overlooked by the public and quickly went out of print. In 1971, however, Neihardt appeared on Dick Cavett's television show, and Black Elk (who had died in 1950) and his spiritual heritage captured the fascination of people around the world.

By now a new generation of missionaries, too, was able to appreciate the book, encouraged by a new and popular respect for the spiritual riches of indigenous religions. Young Sioux today can dance the Sun Dance one week and receive the sacrament of confirmation the next. This syncretism does not diminish either tradition if we recognize with Black Elk that all living things are "children of one mother, and their father is one Spirit."

Black Elk Speaks is an apocalyptic work, covering a period when the tribes of the Great Plains were all but destroyed. The book contains dream sequences, rituals, and stories of pitched battles with the *wasichu* (white people). Of particular importance to Black Elk is the account of his Great Vision when he was nine years old and ill with fever. He felt himself lifted into the sky to meet the "six grandfathers" and was given a stick to plant, which became the tree of life. He also received the multicolored herb of understanding. He dropped the herb onto the earth where it rooted and flowered; light shone from it "so that all creatures saw it, and in no place was there darkness."

We should all have such a vision.

THE SPIRIT OF
MEDIEVAL PHILOSOPHY

(1932 ◆ Philosophy)

ÉTIENNE GILSON

(1884–1978)

Thomas Merton tells the story of a time before his conversion when he impulsively bought a book in Manhattan. On the train back to Long Island he opened it and found to his disgust that it bore an imprimatur. "I felt I had been cheated!" Merton remembered. "They should have warned me that it was a Catholic book. Then I never would have bought it."

As he began to read the book, however, he was impressed by the author's learning and came to grudgingly admit that here was a rich intellectual tradition he knew nothing about. Merton recalled, "The result was that I at once acquired an immense respect for Catholic philosophy and for the Catholic faith."

The book he picked up that day was *The Spirit of Medieval Philosophy* by Étienne Gilson. As a philosopher and historian of philosophy, Gilson was esteemed in Europe and North America. He lectured at Harvard, taught at the Sorbonne and at the Pontifical Institute of Medieval Studies in Toronto. The various chapters of the book had originally been lectures at the University of Aberdeen in Scotland.

In these Gifford Lectures Gilson was responding to the belief, common in his day, that "Christian philosophy" was an oxymoron—a contradiction in terms. Nineteenth-century critics maintained that thinkers of the Middle Ages—Thomas Aquinas, Bonaventure, and Duns Scotus, among them—brought nothing new to philosophy but simply commented on the Greeks.

Gilson takes vigorous exception to that view. He maintains that medieval philosophers, having Christian revelation at their service, made vital corrections to the work of Plato and Aristotle. While the ancients may have understood the notion of prime mover, he said, they never associated it with a Creator who is pure being; and, not grasping the notion of creation, they reached erroneous conclusions about the physical world.

"The spirit of medieval philosophy," says Gilson, "was . . . fruitful and creative in so far as it was willing to be incorporated with a Wisdom that lived itself by faith and Charity. . . ."

It was religious faith that allowed rational philosophy to flourish in the Middle Ages, Gilson claims. "The Middle Ages . . . represented the history of the world as a great poem, which takes on a complete and intelligible meaning as soon as we know the beginning and the end."

Gilson also defends medieval philosophy from attacks at the other end. Humanists such as Luther and Erasmus damned the Scholastics for attending to pagans (i.e., the Greeks). To them, Christian revelation alone is truth. In response Gilson says such allegations, if taken seriously, would be the death of philosophy. He maintains that natural knowledge is essential, even holy, for humans, including Christians. Christ took on human nature and died so that humanity might be glorified.

The Spirit of Medieval Philosophy begins with an overview of the problem. Subsequent chapters take up philosophical topics in which the Middle Ages made major contributions, among them being and its necessity, analogy and causality, anthropology, and free will.

This is not light reading, but neither is it overly burdened with technical terms. To those with a philosophical mind and historical sense, it will bring real pleasure. They will find that Étienne Gilson presented an elegant defense of the philosophy of the Middle Ages and wrote one of the great Catholic books of the twentieth century.

VIPERS' TANGLE

(1932 ✦ Fiction)

FRANÇOIS MAURIAC

(1885–1970)

The old man lies in his sickroom scribbling a letter to his wife. It's a long letter, more like a diary, and recounts the hatred that grew in him over the years for her and their children. Outside his door they stop to listen, then move on. Downstairs they argue in muted voices: Is the old man really dying this time? Will he leave his fortune to us? How much will it be? They are frightened.

Upstairs he writes bitterly, "Most fathers are beloved, but you [my wife] were my enemy, and my children have gone over to the enemy."

He had come from country people, raised by a mother who through shrewd investment had been able to assemble a few valuable properties. She denied him nothing. Yet he was a graceless child, resentful of his dirt beginnings, and he thanked her not at all. As a young man he proposed marriage to the daughter of landed bourgeoisie. They treated him with condescension but, respectful of his potential wealth, agreed to the match.

After their marriage his wife confides in a casual moment that there had been another suitor for her hand, a handsome young man who failed to meet her family's requirements. The husband hears this with inner rage—all his insecurities confirmed. From this moment there grows between them a "Great Silence." He records the whole sad story in this last letter before death.

Vipers' Tangle is that letter. It is a record of an old man's hatreds but also, as he approaches the end, of his attempt to understand them. "I know my heart," he writes, "—it is a knot of vipers. They have almost squeezed the life out of it. They have beslavered it with their poison, but underneath their squirming, it still beats."

Gradually, as we see him going over personal history, trying to decide whether he should pass along his estate to his avaricious children, the old man gains insight into himself. "All through my life I have chosen wrongly," he writes. "I have never learned to live—not in the sense that those of this world understand living. Of the art of life I have, quite literally, known nothing."

To everyone's astonishment, the wife dies before the husband, leaving it up to the children to make sense of the letter and to wonder if, just maybe, deep down, their mother and their father really did love each other.

Some French critics attacked *Vipers' Tangle* when it was first published for the way François Mauriac caricatured the religious values of the French middle class. Indeed, throughout the novel, the old man's skepticism is used as a sharp tool to expose the shallowness of his family's conventional religion.

Mauriac was one of the most distinguished novelists in France during the period between the world wars. His stories often focused on sin, sexuality, and the oppression of provincial life. He had to go into hiding for a while during the Nazi occupation. After the war he became an ardent Gaullist. He was awarded the Nobel Prize for Literature in 1952.

THE DIARY OF A
COUNTRY PRIEST

(1936 ◆ Fiction)

GEORGES BERNANOS

(1888–1948)

We start with a solitary priest, keeping his diary. We never learn his name. He sits in his kitchen, writing by candlelight. He is a simple man of peasant stock, so undistinguished by looks and breeding that his superiors shunted him off to this backwater village in northwestern France. He is desperately lonely; even prayer is difficult. The diary is the place where he unburdens his soul.

This is not to say he is unhappy, if happiness signifies contentment with one's lot. He *is* content. He expected nothing more than this. But the poverty, ignorance, and moral blindness of his people fill him with deep sadness. He wants to call them out of their torpor but doesn't know how, and he feels keenly his own failings as a priest. Villagers talk about him behind his back. He writes, ". . . Sometimes I fancy the village has nailed me up here on a cross and is watching me die."

The Diary of a Country Priest is a window on a man's soul as he carries out his daily ministry, providing for the living and dead, confronting the sinful, healing the distraught, and all the time trying to deal with his own pain—both the existential pain of living with uncertainty and failure and the real, physical one that gnaws at his insides. The reader suspects—long before the priest does—that the pain signals something dreadful.

Georges Bernanos published *The Diary of a Country Priest* in 1936. Ten years earlier his first novel had made him famous, giving him the freedom to leave his job as an insurance inspector. An ardent Frenchman with family roots in Spain, he supported anti-Franco forces in the Spanish Civil War. During World War II he worked on behalf of Charles de Gaulle, his high-school classmate.

Bernanos found writing to be a painful human endeavor. Blank pages terrified him, and he needed to be in public places—railway coaches or coffeehouses—to be creative. He had a deep compassion for suffering humanity, believing that pain and suffering are not the dark underside of human existence but the very stuff of life. At one point his village priest confides in his diary,

> "More and more firmly I am convinced that what we call sadness, anguish, despair, as though to persuade ourselves that these are only states of the Spirit, are the Spirit itself. I believe that ever since his fall, man's condition is such that neither around him nor within him can he perceive anything, except in the form of agony."

While its landscape may be bleak, this *Diary* is far from a depressing experience. We perceive—even though the priest himself does not—that he is a holy person. At times he surprises himself with his ability to see into people's hearts. By the end of the book his vision has sufficiently penetrated the dark crust of the human condition to confirm that underneath "all is grace."

The Diary of a Country Priest is one of the great works of religious fiction in any language or era.

BREAD AND WINE

(1936 ◆ Fiction)

IGNAZIO SILONE

(1900–1978)

Ignazio Silone was an antifascist novelist and agitator during the Mussolini regime in Italy before and during World War II. At first aligning himself with the Communists, Silone later broke with the party. But he never lost his commitment to the poor, especially the rural poor of his native land.

Bread and Wine, Silone's best-known work, tells the story of a leftist agitator who returns to Italy in 1935 after fifteen years in exile. Sick and hunted by the carabinieri, Pietro Spina disguises himself as a priest and finds refuge in a village in the bleak Abruzzi Mountains. He befriends the peasants of Pietrosecca, trying to make them see the ways in which they are being exploited. They are too fatalistic and ground down by poverty to change. "Things always go their own way," one of them tells him, "whether you understand them or not."

When Spina sneaks into Rome to make contact with other members of his shadow organization, the situation is not much better. Old comrades have been killed or tortured by the police. The crushing presence of the police state is everywhere; all the professions, and even the church, have been compromised. Spina is the last idealist left, and even he is disturbed when his international organization seems more interested in rhetoric than in improving the lives of the poor. When the Mussolini government declares war in Africa, the only thing Spina can do is scrawl peace slogans on the walls of buildings. To him it seems a feeble protest.

Because he lost faith in the church, Spina is uncomfortable with his priestly disguise. Still, he discovers people are more comforted by the little blessings he reluctantly performs as a priest than by his political efforts. His old Latin teacher, a retired priest, assures Spina that his feeble activism is holy:

> "'I, too, in the dregs of my afflictions, have asked myself: where is God and why has he abandoned us? Certainly the loudspeakers and bells announcing the new slaughter were not God. Nor were the cannon shots and the bombing of the Ethiopian villages, of which we read every day in the newspapers. But if one poor man gets up in the middle of the night and writes on the walls of the village with a piece of charcoal or varnish, "Down with the War," the presence of God is undoubtedly behind that man.'"

Bread and Wine is a bitter protest against the modern totalitarian state, whether from the right or from the left, and a hymn to the power of dreams, even in difficult times. Silone creates memorable characters and tells his story with humor, vivid local color, and deep compassion. He wrote the novel before World War II, then rewrote it after the war when Mussolini had been defeated—but not to add a note of triumph. Silone has no illusions. He insists that the state can always devour us, the church always betray us, but in spite of that the ideal of peace and brotherhood still has the power to change lives.

THE REED OF GOD

(1944 ◆ Spirituality)

CARYLL HOUSELANDER

(1901–1954)

No pilgrimage through Catholic literature would be complete without a book on Mary. In the twenty-first century, as in the Middle Ages, Mary holds a distinctive place in the Catholic imagination. She is the virgin mother, the faithful disciple, the proto-priest who bore the Lamb of God to the altar of history.

And maybe no one has written more beautifully of Mary than Caryll Houselander, who spent much of her life in London. Houselander was an unusual person—myopic, introverted with moments of zaniness, a chain smoker who fasted like a desert hermit, a professional wood-carver, artist, and something of a mystic. It was said she could see Christ in people, a quality confirmed by a witness as astute as Ronald Knox.

The Reed of God is a meditation on the life of Mary, whom Houselander compared to a reed flute on which God played the tune. As she described it,

> "The reed grows by the streams. It is the simplest of things, but it must be cut by a sharp knife, hollowed out, and the stops must be cut in it; it must be shaped and pierced before it can utter the shepherd's song. It is the narrowest emptiness in the world, but the little reed utters infinite music."

The book opens with a chapter on "emptiness," followed by an insightful reflection on Advent, which Houselander calls "the season of the seed." She gives us a picture of Mary when "the seed of the Bread of Life was in her, [when] the Glory of God was shrined in her darkness." She celebrates the ordinariness of Mary's life in vivid language: "She was forming his body from hers. His flesh and blood. From her humanity, she gave him his humanity. Washing, weaving, kneading, sweeping, her hands prepared his hands for the nails."

Subsequent chapters take us through the life of Christ—the life of Mary—during the boyhood of Jesus, his ministry, death, and resurrection. Houselander is devout in an earthy rather than a pious way; she emphasizes the gritty reality of the incarnation and urges readers to meet God through their own bodies and in the messiness of daily living.

Her portrait of Mary frequently has the crucifixion in the background. Writing during World War II, she contemplates a world geared up for killing, where children "pull their rags around their starved bodies and compose themselves to die." She adds, "I sit here in a bombed city and say that because a girl surrendered herself to God two thousand years ago . . . everyone [can be] a bearer of Christ into the world."

She compares losing the child Jesus in the Temple to a "loss of God experience"—a painful but purifying part of every person's life. Similarly, the Assumption of Mary becomes in Houselander's view a natural closure, as Mary's body once again is united with her son's: Advent redux.

The Reed of God is a short book, but one brimming with insights and arresting images. It continues to be a fitting representative of Marian literature in our own day.

BRIDESHEAD REVISITED

(1945 ◆ Fiction)

EVELYN WAUGH

(1903–1966)

B*rideshead Revisited* is an enthralling novel, part spoof, part aristocratic soap opera that, underneath it all, has earnest intentions. Just when Evelyn Waugh convinces you that life is a bowl of cherries he takes them away, one by one, and suggests that the empty bowl is God's will.

The story unfolds as a recollection by Charles Ryder who, as a young man at Oxford, becomes friendly with Sebastian Flyte, the titled son of the Marchmain family whose seat is the country estate known as Brideshead. Ryder, a Londoner and only son, is entranced by Sebastian and his exotic family—exotic to Charles because they are Catholic and he is convinced that Catholicism and all religion is a lot of "bosh." Charles and Sebastian live an arcadian existence, toying with art and studies, lounging around Brideshead, and drinking excessively. As it turns out, Charles could leave drink alone when he needed to; Sebastian could not.

Sebastian drinks to escape the critical eye of his mother, Lady Marchmain, regarded by many to be a saint but whose unbending rectitude caused her husband to flee and now weighs heavily on her children. It makes Sebastian increasingly self-destructive and drives his sister Julia into an unhappy marriage. Charles, too, is sent packing from Brideshead for supporting Sebastian against his mother.

Time passes. Charles Ryder, now a successful artist, encounters Julia during an Atlantic crossing. Both of them are trapped in unhappy marriages. They fall in love and move back into Brideshead,

Lady Marchmain having died. But now Charles faces the full force of the family's Catholic faith—or, as Julia puts it, with "Death, Judgment, Heaven, Hell, Nanny Hawkins, and the Catechism." Although she loves him, she is tormented by guilt for living with Charles. At length he must deal with the fact that her religious faith is more than an ornament but has consequences.

Evelyn Waugh, whose books were acclaimed for their craft and high style, became a Catholic in his late twenties. His Catholicism, though, was aristocratic in texture and inclination—a quality clearly evident in *Brideshead Revisited*.

The targets of his satire are bourgeois industrialists, politicians, and similar "men on the make." For example, Julia describes her first husband, a politician, as "a sort of primitive savage, but he was something absolutely modern and up-to-date that only this ghastly age could produce. A tiny bit of a man pretending to be whole."

It is this desire for wholeness in people and in society that gives Waugh's fiction a deep seriousness that transcends snobbery. For Waugh the Christian religion is culture's backbone. It forces us to stand up straight when we would rather slouch. And it gives us dreams.

Late in the book Charles recalls how he once came across Julia sitting by herself in a "magical sadness" which seemed to say, "Surely, I was made for some other purpose than this."

If you think Waugh lays this on a little thick, you are not alone. George Orwell called Waugh "as good a writer as it is possible to be while holding untenable positions."

But in the end Waugh's world is so complete and compelling that you might just accept it—pious phrases, snobbery, and all. Read *Brideshead Revisited* and see if you don't agree.

THE SEVEN STOREY MOUNTAIN

(1948 ✦ Autobiography)

THOMAS MERTON

(1915–1968)

T *he Seven Storey Mountain* first appeared in public on October 4, 1948. Initially, booksellers were not sure what to do with this autobiography of a Trappist monk. They placed a few copies on back-of-the-store shelves devoted to "Catholic" books. Its publisher, Harcourt, Brace and Company, was as uncertain as the bookstores. A first printing of 5,000 copies had been planned, but when prepublication endorsements came from Graham Greene and Evelyn Waugh, the printing was bumped up to 7,500. Then three book clubs picked it up. A second printing of 20,000 copies was ordered even before the first appeared. By Christmas stacks of *The Seven Storey Mountain* were displayed at store entrances, and Harcourt, Brace was astonished to learn that 2,000 copies were being bought each day. By the end of 1949, 600,000 copies of the English-language hardback edition had been printed, and a dozen translations were in the works.

Why was *The Seven Storey Mountain* such a publishing phenomenon in postwar America, and why is the book still significant today? For one reason, Thomas Merton spoke in a distinctive American voice, accessible to all readers, whatever their religious or cultural background. He was a cultured man who knew art and poetry, but who also liked jazz, flirted with Communism, corresponded in doubletalk with his friends, and was something of a jokester. The range of his interests fascinated readers in the early 1950s who tended to see all Catholics as blue-collar laborers.

Then there was the book itself—the account of a thoroughly modern, sophisticated individual who turned his back on the twentieth century to enter an exotic community of monks hidden away in the hills of western Kentucky. Merton's life journey had a powerful countercultural allure. Here was a man acquainted with Freudian psychology who could still talk seriously about sin, penance, and God. To a people wearied of war yet armed with atomic weapons and living with the uncertainty of a new cold war, Merton spoke of simplicity of heart and the need for faith.

In structure, *The Seven Storey Mountain* is a straightforward narrative that recounts Merton's life from childhood to his early days at Gethsemane Abbey. It tells of the death of his mother when Merton was six, how he was taken from America to France by his artist father, and his education at schools in France and England. Forced to withdraw from Cambridge University because of carousing, Merton came back to New York, entered Columbia University, and began a gradual religious conversion that led to his baptism in the Catholic church and eventually to a religious vocation.

The work was written when Merton was a young monk and contains pious passages that made him uncomfortable years later. Yet there is an undeniable energy and authenticity to the account. After writing it he was forced by superiors to delete sections that detailed his young, dissolute life, with the result that the guilt he expresses on its pages seems excessive to contemporary readers. Biographies that have appeared since Merton's death in 1968 correct the record.

Thomas Merton wrote numerous books in his lifetime—histories, journals, spirituality, poetry—and all of them are fascinating. But for anyone who wants to know Merton and the age he lived in, *The Seven Storey Mountain* is a seminal work.

RELIGION AND THE RISE
OF WESTERN CULTURE

(1949 ✦ History)

CHRISTOPHER DAWSON

(1889–1970)

One often hears unbelievers say that while they cannot accept the doctrinal part of Christianity, its creeds and beliefs, they do admire its art—and they will go on about cathedrals and Gregorian chant and Byzantine icons. Historian Christopher Dawson would have responded that the two cannot be separated: art springs from faith and speaks the language of faith. Indeed, he goes further, and argues that nearly all of Western culture, its social institutions as well as its learning and art, was first planted by the Christian church in the soil of Europe and nurtured there until it took root.

He makes that case most convincingly in *Religion and the Rise of Western Culture*, a work that he first delivered as lectures in 1948–49. His message is still timely. More recently Pope John Paul II and Pope Benedict XVI have echoed Dawson's point and warned that by its rapid movement toward secularization Europe runs the risk of losing its soul.

Dawson was a Welsh-born scholar who became a Catholic in his mid-twenties and who taught at Harvard and universities in Britain. He preferred to call himself a "metahistorian"—neither a historian, strictly speaking, nor a theologian—but interested in the big questions that link history and culture.

His book tells the story of the church in Europe from the breakdown of the Roman Empire through the thirteenth century. In his view the church played a vital role in civilizing the first wave of barbarians who attacked Rome and a subsequent wave of Norsemen and Magyars. Missionary bishops learned to deal with warrior kings, in some cases presiding at their coronations, thereby giving the church leverage with uncivilized tribes.

Much of the civilizing influence of the church in Europe was provided by monasteries. Monks came from the British Isles to reclaim continental Europe for Christianity after the first barbarian invasions. (That story is told elsewhere by Thomas Cahill in *How the Irish Saved Civilization.*) Dawson also relates how the Cluniac monks preserved order following the collapse of the Carolingian Empire. Being autonomous entities, monasteries had the freedom and flexibility to adapt new strategies to cope with tumultuous times.

As the so-called Dark Ages gave way to the Middle Ages, cathedral schools eventually sprang up in principal cities, teaching not only religious subjects but also poetry, classics, and civil law. Aristotle and the Greek philosophers were rediscovered. Supported by the church, universities were founded in Paris and Bologna, then other cities, leading to the formation of professional, educated classes.

According to Dawson, the church also played a role in the development of cities, which gradually replaced medieval manors as centers of population. And with the cities came the growth of sophisticated trade. Guilds and communes were inspired by the spirit of collective living embedded in church structures.

Dawson makes the point that in medieval times Europe passed through repeated reforms—the Middle Ages were far from being static. Revolutionary idealism was a hallmark of the thirteenth century, giving rise to armed revolts in the new city-states, but also bringing forth St. Francis, St. Dominic, and their friars.

The eight hundred years of the Middle Ages constituted a stirring, dynamic era, and in this erudite book Christopher Dawson brings it all back to life.

WAITING FOR GOD

(1950 ◆ Spirituality)

SIMONE WEIL

(1909–1943)

It seems to me that the will of God is that I should not enter the Church at present." So writes a French woman to a priest friend in January 1942. The war is raging. She is Jewish and must flee France. Yet the issue that totally engages these two people is whether she should be baptized. The priest urges her to take the step. She resists. She writes, "I feel that it is necessary and ordained that I should be alone, a stranger and exile in relation to every human circle without exception."

This woman who desired to be an exile and stranger was Simone Weil, a modern mystic. She was a teacher of philosophy who, earlier in life, had left her position at a girls' high school to take a menial factory job in order to share the hardships of the workers. When she fled France to escape the Nazis, she went to Morocco, then New York, then to London to join the French Resistance. There she declined to take her full food ration because she wanted to be in solidarity with the people of occupied France. She wrote hopeful essays about the postwar world, but her many privations accelerated her ill health. At the age of thirty-four she died of tuberculosis, an outcast to the end.

Simone Weil was born of Jewish parents but laid claim to a "Christian soul" from earliest childhood. As an adult she spent Holy Week at a Benedictine monastery "where the passion of Christ entered into my being once and for all." She was a passion-ate outcast who wanted to embrace the whole world and who feared that joining a church that claimed to be an exclusive church might restrict that passion. She wrote, "In my eyes Christianity is catholic by right but not in fact. So many things are outside of it, so many things that I love and do not want to give up, so many things that God loves, otherwise they would not be in existence."

Waiting for God is a collection of letters and other writings dating from the time that Weil was claiming her Christianity and yet resisting the church. She felt she belonged to a larger church. Assembled after her death, the letters reveal her as a person of painful honesty and absolute commitment to her vocation as she perceived it. Weil believed unquestionably that her life was lived in obedience to God. She understood that hers was to be a life of suffering and exile. As she explained,

> "If it cannot be given to me to deserve the Cross of Christ, at least may I share that of the good thief. Of all the beings other than Christ of whom the Gospel tells us, the good thief is the one I most envy. To have been at the side of Christ and in the same state during the crucifixion seems to me a far more enviable privilege than to be at the right hand of his glory."

The volume also contains Weil's perceptive commentary on the Our Father as well as an essay on the "implicit love of God" which, in many ways, anticipates Karl Rahner's notion of the anonymous Christian.

Even though she never formally converted, Simone Weil's *Waiting for God* is a most eloquent Catholic book.

THE END OF THE MODERN WORLD

(1950 ✦ *Philosophy*)

ROMANO GUARDINI

(1885–1968)

According to philosophers and social critics, our world has reached an age of "postmodernism," which promises to have profound effects on politics, art, social structures, and human consciousness generally. The underlying structures of postmodernism are still not understood by the average person, but more than fifty years ago theologian Romano Guardini wrote a remarkably prescient book that put it in historical perspective and warned of its possible effects.

Guardini was an Italian-born priest raised in Mainz, Germany, who taught for many years at the University of Munich. He was internationally known in the years leading up to Vatican II, the author of scores of books that influenced many budding theologians, among them Karl Rahner and Joseph Ratzinger.

In *The End of the Modern World*, Guardini outlines what he sees as the four ages of European culture. The first was the classical age of the Greeks and Romans—insular and wise, but incomplete. The second age arrived with Christianity which supplied faith as an organizing principle and envisioned nature, knowledge, and human society together under God's dominion.

This period lasted through the Middle Ages, but with the Renaissance came the first stirrings of the modern age. It introduced the scientific mind that sought to measure, calculate, and control nature, but which also, as a result, separated humans and nature. The natural world was now an object to be studied. The modern age believed in cause and effect and in progress. The earth and the heavens lay ready for exploring. Skepticism and curiosity replaced faith. God became increasingly irrelevant.

Nationalism, industrialization, two world wars, the Holocaust, and the atomic bomb put an end to the optimism of the modern world. Writing in 1950, under the shadow of nuclear annihilation, Guardini states, "Many men now suspected that 'culture' is not at all what the modern age thought it to be; many suspect that culture is not the realm of beautiful security but a game of dice. Its stakes are life and death, but nobody knows how the last die will be cast."

In our new postmodern age progress is no longer certain, earth and the heavens no longer unlimited, cause and effect no longer in force. Crazy things happen. Guardini didn't live to see September 11, but he would have understood it.

Guardini doesn't offer solutions. He talks vaguely about the need for a "contemplative spirit" and a "new asceticism." Above all, he says, humans must awaken to a new experience of depth, be obedient to a moral vision and attentive to God's revelation.

The End of the Modern World is prophetic but also a creature of its time and place. The book is limited by its Eurocentric view. Guardini was not sensitive to people around the globe who didn't go through these stages, nor does he explore the possibility of Christianity working with other faiths. In most aspects, though, his analysis still seems fresh and new and has been confirmed by events in the years since he wrote it.

ENTHUSIASM

(1950 ✦ Theology)

RONALD A. KNOX

(1888–1957)

The Christian church, through history, has been like a whirling globe, forever spinning off factions by the force of its turning even as it draws elements back into orthodoxy by the force of gravity. Patterns repeat themselves. The same mind-set that threatened the Corinthian community in the first century also infiltrated eighteenth-century Protestantism and continues, to some extent, among modern-day evangelicals. Ronald Knox calls this tendency "enthusiasm"—a belief that true religion is more spirit than flesh, that God speaks to persons rather than to churches, and that it is more important to "feel close" to God than to theologize about him. Knox's book by that title is the definitive treatment of the phenomenon.

Knox claims there are two sorts of religious enthusiasts, the mystical and the evangelical. The mystical enthusiast concentrates almost exclusively on the God within, believing that union with the indwelling God ought to be the focus of religion. The evangelical enthusiast, on the other hand, is more conscious of humankind's fallen nature. Being forgiven and becoming a new creature in God's sight is what really matters. For both the mystical and the evangelical enthusiast, however, religion is a me-and-God proposition. Neither of them requires an institutional church dispensing sacraments and bonding believers to each other and to the great mass of humanity. For the enthusiasts it is enough just to "be with" God.

Enthusiasm is a large work—more than five hundred pages of historical detail that surveys enthusiastic movements in the New

Testament, early heretical groups such as the Montanists and Donatists, medieval Albigensians, as well as Quakers, Jansenists, Quietists, Moravians, Methodists, and Shakers among others. Going from Marcion to Mary Baker Eddy is quite a ride.

And Ronald A. Knox, the author, was quite a person. As a young man he converted to Catholicism (shocking his father, the Anglican bishop of Manchester), was ordained a priest, and subsequently became chaplain to Catholic undergraduates at Oxford University. Knox wrote numerous detective novels, religious books (e.g., *The Mass in Slow Motion, The Creed in Slow Motion*), and, at the request of the English hierarchy, single-handedly translated the Latin Bible into English. His posthumous biography was written by Evelyn Waugh.

Many believe that *Enthusiasm* was Knox's most enduring achievement because the phenomenon it explores is everpresent in Christian communities. In the book Knox confesses that he feels a personal attraction to the enthusiast who "because he exaggerates, always has our sympathies in a given encounter. He cuts a finer figure, doing nothing by halves." Enthusiasts like François Fénelon and John Wesley, he says, "impose their personalities on you"; their opponents "are more depressing figures by comparison." But, he adds, enthusiasms eventually fade, and the opponents of enthusiasm—although dull and uninteresting—are more likely to preserve the enduring core of belief.

THE END OF THE AFFAIR

(1951 ◆ Fiction)

GRAHAM GREENE

(1904–1991)

Is it possible to be a sinner and saint at the same time? A lover and a hater? A believer and a nonbeliever? These are some of the questions that will run through your mind when you read *The End of the Affair*, a novel by a man who never liked being pigeon-holed as a "Catholic novelist." Based on Graham Greene's own relationship with a married woman, the story is a searing record of the obsession, desire, jealousy, passion, guilt, and often the grief, that pervades love affairs.

It may also be a record of faith and human growth. Greene suggests as much when he quotes Léon Bloy at the beginning of the book: "Man has places in his heart which do not exist, and into them enters suffering in order that they may have existence."

In the novel Maurice Bendrix, a writer, falls in love with Sara Miles, the wife of a government official. The time and place is wartime London. Death is in the air as the lovers meet at her place or his. One afternoon a bomb strikes his building when they are in it. Bendrix lies injured, perhaps dying, and Sara promises secretly that she will end the affair if only God will let him live. When he does survive, she leaves him. Bendrix is devastated.

Now Bendrix hates Sara, thinking she has left him for another lover. Sara, although equally lonely, has at least been given what she asked for, and she begins to move closer to this mysterious God who answers prayers. At last Bendrix discovers the truth by reading her personal diary, secured with the help of a private detective. He turns his hate on God, his rival for her favors. But how can he hate

God? Bendrix has never believed in God, and to hate God he would have to acknowledge God's existence. How his hate and their love are resolved is part of *The End of the Affair.*

Graham Greene was a journalist and foreign correspondent who worked in the intelligence department of the British Foreign Office during World War II. Many of his works became films, including *The Third Man, Our Man in Havana,* and *The Quiet American.*

Greene's principal characters are usually tormented figures, caught up in great world events and trapped by the consequences of personal choices. Rarely, in his novels, does religious faith serve as a consolation; more often it is a challenge, a complication, a question rather than an answer. Always keeping a skeptical distance, Greene—like his character Bendrix—nevertheless gives God a grudging place. One is never sure at the end of his books whether the miraculous has occurred or forgiveness has been received. Maybe so, maybe not. It is nothing more than a possibility, but a possibility that, when we reflect on it, plunges us into mystery.

THE LONG LONELINESS

(1952 ✦ Autobiography)

DOROTHY DAY

(1897–1980)

Conversion stories have always had a special place in Catholic literature. Over the centuries, beginning with St. Augustine, those who have responded to the call to change their lives utterly have felt compelled to tell us why, driven by the passion of their new faith. We, in turn, have listened, fascinated. What could be more dramatic than Francis shucking off the power (not to mention the clothing) of his father and setting off to become the poor brother of Assisi?

The twentieth century put a unique twist on the conversion story, as scores and then thousands of persons lost faith in Communism and rediscovered belief in democracy and God. Thomas Merton toyed with Communism. Writers like Arthur Koestler, Ignazio Silone, Richard Wright, Whittaker Chambers, and Stephen Spender did more than toy. And then there is Dorothy Day, a case unto herself. While she embraced God and the Catholic church, Dorothy Day never lost her commitment to the poor, the masses, or to radicalism as a means of reform.

As she tells it in *The Long Loneliness*, Dorothy was the daughter of an itinerant journalist who worked for big-city papers in Chicago, San Francisco, and New York. The family never had much money, but she scraped together enough to attend the University of Illinois for two years. Then she who had learned socialism by reading Upton Sinclair and Leo Tolstoy found work as a writer for radical newspapers in New York.

Her book describes years of struggle. She was a passionate defender of labor unions and working people. She went to jail demonstrating for women's rights. She had an unhappy love affair. During all this time she sensed a relationship with God that blew hot and cold. Radical friends laughed when she went into churches to pray, but Dorothy Day was undeterred.

The turning point came when she bore a daughter, Tamar, and found deep happiness. She recalls, "My very experience as a radical, my whole make-up, led me to want to associate myself with others, with the masses, in loving and praising God." She was determined to have her daughter baptized—but where? To her the Catholic church "claimed and held the allegiance of the masses of people in all the cities where I had lived. They poured in and out of her doors on Sundays and holy days, for novenas and missions." So Dorothy's daughter received her baptism in a Catholic church, and she herself was baptized some months later, in December 1927.

The rest of her story is better known—her meeting with Peter Maurin and the beginnings of the Catholic Worker movement in the early 1930s. They founded houses of hospitality in urban slums and published *The Catholic Worker* newspaper that sells, still today, for a penny a copy.

While Day is reticent in *The Long Loneliness* about her private life, she is candid about her faith story. She tells how she found within Catholicism a radicalism to match her own—a faith that supports workers and pacifism, a church of the poor and of social justice. First she was converted, and then she worked to convert the church to the teaching at the heart of the gospel.

THE PHENOMENON OF MAN

(1955 ◆ Spirituality)

PIERRE TEILHARD DE CHARDIN

(1881–1955)

The eighteenth-century Enlightenment drove a wedge between science and faith, leaving both of those human activities deeply wounded. Cut loose from the realm of the rational, organized faith drifted toward irrelevance and reaction. For its part science lost the living connection it had with value and meaning systems and so gave rise to mindless technology, war, and social disorder. Recent decades have been marked by some recovery of the essential link between science and faith. Probably no person has contributed more to this movement than Pierre Teilhard de Chardin, a priest who was also a scientist, whose definitive work came under such a cloud it could not be published in his lifetime.

Teilhard (he is usually referred to by the first part of his family name) was raised in southern France, the fourth of eleven children. From his youth he was drawn to a love of nature, collecting stones and metal artifacts. This was coupled with a strong religious devotion. He entered the Society of Jesus in 1899. While with the Jesuits he studied paleontology, and later did field studies in Egypt and the Far East. In China he was involved in the discovery and identification of Peking Man, whose bones most scientists accept as an early humanoid.

Born the year before Charles Darwin died, Teilhard accepted evolution as the explanation for change in nature. In writings that culminated with *The Phenomenon of Man*, he theorized that not only did the earth and living beings evolve, human consciousness evolved as well. He called this realm of consciousness the "noosphere," and in his view the noosphere, along with biological life, is being drawn to ever-higher states, until eventually it reaches the "omega point"—that point outside of space and time at which God becomes one with creation.

The Phenomenon of Man is neither science nor theology, but a personal synthesis of the two that is a mystical commentary on the workings of nature. Because Teilhard was given to grand, sweeping statements using newly coined words, church authorities were predictably uneasy with his work. His application of evolutionary processes to social and intellectual movements is still hotly contested. However, as a piece of prophetic writing the book has been a major influence on the environmental movement and on the reconciliation of science and faith. A committed evolutionist, Teilhard would not have accepted the intelligent design theory being advanced by some today. Yet he did find God in the natural world—a richly incarnate God, abiding in matter, moving and fostering its development, leaving traces of divinity in all things.

Teilhard was refused permission by religious superiors to publish *The Phenomenon of Man* during his lifetime. He was barred from teaching and asked to make his home outside France. He spent his last years in the United States, dying suddenly in New York City on Easter Sunday, 1955. *Le Phénomène Humain* was published in France later that year; the English-language edition appeared in 1959.

THE LORD OF THE RINGS

(1954–1955 ✦ Fiction)

J. R. R. TOLKIEN

(1892–1973)

This trilogy of novels written by an Oxford professor in the 1940s seems destined to become a treasure of world literature. Countless readers around the world have claimed it as their favorite fictional work. American hippies championed it back in the 1970s, and more recently the Peter Jackson films have put a lock on its reputation.

How does one account for the popularity of *The Lord of the Rings?* Its success surprised its author. Even its champions concede it is not a great work of art. However the epic appealed to readers living in the decades after World War II when global corporations worked hand in glove with governments to put the squeeze on ordinary people. It seemed to many people that fighting this dark power was too great an undertaking for ordinary folk. But not for a hobbit by the name of Frodo.

To tell his story John Ronald Reuel Tolkien invented an entire imaginary world, fleshed it out with believable characters, and put them in combat with an implacable foe. Although personally he was Catholic, there is no religion in the make-believe world of Middle Earth. Still, in a letter to a friend, Tolkien called his trilogy "a fundamentally religious and Catholic work; unconsciously so at first, but consciously in the revision . . . The religious element is absorbed into the story and the symbolism."

Tolkien intended to write one novel, but his English publisher complained about the size of the project and opted to bring it out in three volumes. In *The Fellowship of the Ring* the hobbit Bilbo Baggins gives an enchanted ring to his innocent nephew Frodo. It is the One Ring that gives its wearer immense power but inevitably corrupts him. Frodo doesn't realize its import, but Gandalf the wizard does and launches Frodo and his friend Sam on a journey to destroy the ring and rid Middle Earth of evil.

In *The Two Towers* the tale picks up speed. Frodo, Sam, and their companions break up into three parties, one of which is captured. The others attempt a rescue but encounter the evil wizard Saruman who resides in the dark tower of Orthanc. The novel has fierce battles as well as quiet moments when the characters and their relationships are delicately fleshed out.

Frodo's journey comes to a dramatic conclusion in *The Return of the King.* The guardianship of the ring has fallen to the little people, many of them outcasts, who sense the hopelessness of their cause yet find strength to continue. In the end, as in real life, their triumph is mixed with sadness as the world they inhabited at the beginning is ruined for them.

Tolkien was an old-fashioned believer in whose world right and wrong were locked into bitter warfare. He himself was a soldier who had fought at the Somme in World War I and who wrote *The Lord of the Rings* during World War II when England was fighting for its very life. His friend the poet W. H. Auden observed that depicting war between good and evil is always a "ticklish business" for writers, since good can't impose itself by force without ceasing to be good. Still, Auden felt Tolkien handled the matter better than John Milton did. The forces of good always have the advantage of imagination—they can see that evil is a blind trap—whereas the forces of evil have no insight into the good. And Tolkien used imagination to his—and therefore our—great advantage.

A GOOD MAN IS HARD TO FIND

(1955 ✦ Fiction)

FLANNERY O'CONNOR

(1925–1964)

Flannery O'Connor had the unusual experience of growing up Catholic in rural Georgia, and everything she wrote flowed out of the tension between place and faith. Her stories are populated by grotesque characters—criminals, preachers, carnival freaks, dirt-poor farmers, and a few genteel women to make it interesting. But just beneath the surface of these odd, sometimes appalling, and often hilarious stories there flows a river of grace. God is never far away—he just chooses strange ways to make himself known.

In her brief writing career—she died of lupus at the age of thirty-nine—O'Connor published two novels and two collections of stories. Her first collection, *A Good Man Is Hard to Find*, established her in the front rank of American short-story writers and sounded all of her familiar themes.

The title story describes how a family on vacation crosses the path of a serial killer. The grandmother who recognizes him from his wanted poster naively blurts out his name, which settles their fate. But she also senses the killer's infantile confusion and exclaims, "Why you're one of my babies" in the instant before she is shot.

The typical O'Connor plot describes how a character's carefully manicured self-image can suddenly crumble. In "A Stroke of Good Fortune," a married woman, happy to have escaped her dirt-farm origins and its onerous cycle of childbearing, becomes completely unraveled when she realizes she is pregnant. In "The Artificial

Nigger," a rural grandfather sets out to show the big city to his grandson but then denies his relationship to the boy out of fear of the police. The old man, who had imagined himself a wise and faithful mentor, is undone by his act of betrayal.

O'Connor had a sharp eye for class distinctions and the misunderstandings that arise from them. She liked to pit shrewd country folk against educated people who initially patronize them, only to get their comeuppance in the end. It is the kind of reversal in fortune that Jesus used in his parables: the poor will inherit the earth. For instance, in "Good Country People," a Bible salesman gulls a woman with a PhD out of her wooden leg. There are more tragic consequences in "The River," when the young son of shallow urbanite parents attends a riverbank baptism with his babysitter. Sensing a kind of wholehearted acceptance there that he cannot find at home, the boy later goes back alone, and drowns.

Some readers may wonder what grace there is in drowning. But O'Connor, who once described herself as a "hillbilly Thomist," believed that grace is everywhere, even in confusion, and surely in death. For instance, in "The Artificial Nigger," on their way back to the country the grandfather and the boy have an experience that brings them together again, obliterating the old man's betrayal. The grandfather at that moment comes to know the meaning of mercy. As O'Connor describes it,

> "He realized that he was forgiven for sins from the beginning of time, when he had conceived in his own heart the sin of Adam, until the present, when he had denied poor Nelson [the grandson]. He saw that no sin was too monstrous for him to claim as his own, and since God loved in proportion as He forgave, he felt ready at that instant to enter Paradise."

PRISON WRITINGS

(1958　✦　*Spirituality*)

ALFRED DELP

(1907–1945)

On February 2, 1945, Alfred Delp was taken from his jail cell in Plötzensee prison in Berlin to another room where he was hanged by Nazi authorities. He had been arrested initially for plotting against the life of Adolf Hitler, but that charge was dropped at his trial. The most serious charge the court could prove was that Delp and other Christian leaders were planning for a post-Nazi era in Germany.

But what really infuriated the Nazi judge was the fact that Delp was a Jesuit. The judge offered to commute the sentence if Delp would leave the Society of Jesus. Delp refused.

The writings that make up this book were produced in the six months that Alfred Delp was awaiting trial and then execution. A pen and paper were smuggled in for him by the prison's Lutheran chaplain, and his writings smuggled out with the prison laundry. There are a few letters to friends, a few pages from his diary, some meditations on the Advent season and comments on the future of humanity and the church. The writings were published in Germany in 1958 and reprinted many times. The English edition came out in 1962.

Take his reflection on Epiphany, 1945, as an example. He does not mention it in his writing, but this was the last day he celebrated the eucharist, alone in his cell, using bread and wine also smuggled in to him. Delp could easily have used the day to weigh the cruelty of sovereigns who slaughter innocents, but his focus is on interior transformation. "During these long weeks of confinement," he writes, "I have learned by personal experience that a person is truly lost, is the victim of circumstances and oppression only when he is incapable of a great inner sense of depth and freedom."

This notion keeps repeating over and over in Delp's reflections: The flawed social system is not the worst part—the real tragedy is that individuals have lost the sense of God penetrating their world. People are waiting for a star, he says, "and not a glimmer of a star appears because their eyes are blind and cannot see."

One disorienting aspect of these final writings is that Delp approached his death during Advent and Christmas. The time of new beginnings and new life was the end-time for him. He uses it as an opportunity to reconfirm his hope in the future:

> "On the grey horizon eventually light will dawn. The foreground is very obtrusive . . . but it does not really amount to much. The things that really matter are farther off—there conditions are different. The woman has conceived a child, has carried it in her womb and has brought forth a son and thereby the world has passed under a new law. . . . It is a symbol of the new order of things that affects the whole of our life and every phase of our being."

Earlier in life Delp had earned a degree in philosophy and published a book on Martin Heidegger. He had a large view of things. He took time in his last months to reflect on the future role of the church and the need for education. He could also be tender in his care for others, begging forgiveness for hurts he may have caused, thanking his brother Jesuits for their "goodness and loyalty and help."

The prison writings of Alfred Delp still have the power to move and inspire.

A CANTICLE FOR LEIBOWITZ

(1959 ✦ Fiction)

WALTER M. MILLER, JR.

(1923–1996)

As *A Canticle for Leibowitz* opens, it is a thousand years after the Flame Deluge, which swept across the earth when wise men created weapons of war and put them in the hands of unwise princes. Most of the world was destroyed. The few survivors turned against learning, killing the educated and destroying all the written records that could be found. It was the era of Simplification. A few men of learning found refuge in monasteries where the dim light of literacy was preserved. Monks copied old twentieth-century texts and memorized others, often without knowing what they were reading.

One day Brother Francis of the Albertian Order of Leibowitz comes across ancient documents half buried in rubble. One document seems to bear the signature of Isaac Edward Leibowitz, the order's founder. Another contains the words, "pound pastrami, can kraut, six bagels—bring home to Emma."

Brother Francis ponders the words—as do the abbot and all the monks in the monastery. Obviously this is a holy text, but what do the words signify? Blessed Leibowitz is being considered for canonization. Could this be the definitive evidence of sanctity?

In case you think Walter Miller is making fun of the Catholic faith, he is not. He is deadly serious. In this apocalyptic science fiction novel, history repeats itself—after a nuclear war, the world goes through a new dark age. The church, as before, preserves the light of culture, and as before mixes myths in with its accumulated facts.

After the story of Brother Francis and the mysterious documents, which comprises the first third of Miller's book, he moves on to a later age when electricity is harnessed and the human race discovers anew its capacity for organized warfare. By the final third of the book a brand-new global war is heating up, so the monks climb into a spaceship, declare *sic transit mundus*, and blast off in search of a newer and hopefully more peaceful earth.

A Canticle for Leibowitz is an original, sometimes funny, and decidedly bleak view of human history. Jews, too, come in for their share of disappointment. A Jewish hermit reappears throughout the novel, forever seeking the Messiah and never finding him. Eventually he defines the Messiah as the One-Who-Isn't-Coming.

Miller has affectionate regard for monks and religious idealists. Their innocent willingness to believe, for example, that an electrical wiring diagram is a religious icon simply makes them more lovable. It's the politicians and technocrats, the ones who twist knowledge into weapons of war, who are the real villains in the world according to Leibowitz.

Walter Miller's novel won the Hugo Award for science fiction writing and was a great popular success when it first appeared. It was the only novel he ever wrote. Miller was an airman during World War II and took part in the bombing of Monte Cassino Monastery in Italy—an event that had a profound effect on him. He became a Catholic two years after the war. The end of his life was marked by disappointment and sadness. His book, though, has remained a minor classic.

WE HOLD THESE TRUTHS

(1960 ✦ Philosophy)

JOHN COURTNEY MURRAY

(1904–1967)

N ot all authors of great books are necessarily great prose stylists. Let it be said at the outset that *We Hold These Truths* is not a work of art, if beautiful language is the measure. John Courtney Murray, a Jesuit priest, was trained as a theologian but was really a philosopher at heart, and his writing bears the marks of philosophical habit: distinctions carefully made, points one, two, three clearly enumerated, frequent references to underlying principles (in Latin). His text is dense, his argument subtle.

Yet this is the book that made Murray famous, put him on the cover of *Time* magazine, and won him recognition as Catholic America's foremost intellectual. It was published two years before Vatican II opened. Murray was still under a Vatican cloud, forbidden to write about religious liberty, so he confined himself in this book to questions dealing with the American consensus and what it signified.

For his title Murray borrowed four words from the Declaration of Independence and asked whether they could still be spoken with confidence. Who is this "we"? What "truths" do we hold in common, and how do we hold them? Murray believed the consensus formulated by America's founding fathers was falling apart because modernity itself was under attack. The modern era, beginning with the Enlightenment, had removed religion from its role as the arbiter of morality and replaced it with the individual conscience. But conscience had proven not to be up to the task.

Forty years later, we can see how prescient Murray was: America is ever more polarized along cultural and ideological lines. How can we find our way back to consensus again?

For Murray the way back is through natural law, which he felt offers a *via media* for competing factions. Natural law assumes that some laws are basic and fundamental to human nature, that people are intelligent and reality is intelligible. It asks the larger questions. Civil law may ask whether an action is legal; natural law asks whether it is just. It assumes the sacredness and dignity of the individual person. For Murray, natural law—unlike the radical demands of the gospel—may be insufficient to lead a person to sanctity, but it is enough to secure human fulfillment and social peace.

We Hold These Truths was assembled from articles and lectures that were carefully stitched together by Murray and Philip Scharper, his editor at Sheed & Ward. They produced a well-integrated book. The first section looks at issues of pluralism and consensus in the American proposition. The second section is devoted to unsettled questions regarding schools, censorship, and human values. The final section weighs religious and social doctrines that touch on war and national security.

John Courtney Murray practically invented the discipline of "public philosophy," defined by him as the "common universe of discourse in which public issues can be intelligibly stated and intelligently argued." He ended his life being vindicated by Vatican II on the subject of religious liberty and was much honored by his colleagues. Today the highest honor bestowed by the Catholic Theological Society of America is the John Courtney Murray Award.

THE MOVIEGOER

(1961 ✦ Fiction)

WALKER PERCY

(1916–1990)

Binx Bolling lives a life of quiet desperation in the New Orleans suburb of Gentilly. He runs a small brokerage office, has the usual credit cards, subscribes to *Consumer Reports*, and sits erect in a straight-backed chair to watch television in his rented rooms. In the evening he takes a bus to the movie theater where he can envy the easy self-assurance of William Holden or Rory Calhoun. By arranging his world carefully, he keeps at bay the malaise that threatens his soul.

Walker Percy leaned on the works of Jean-Paul Sartre and Søren Kierkegaard when he wrote *The Moviegoer*, an existential novel set in midcentury America. For Binx Bolling, the fantasy world of movies is less phony than the real world with its shallowness and deceit. Speaking directly to the reader, he acknowledges his talent for crap detection: "Now in the thirty-first year of my dark pilgrimage on this earth and knowing less than I ever knew before, having learned only to recognize merde when I see it," he is fated to live in a world where "one hundred percent of people are humanists and ninety-eight percent believe in God, and men are dead, dead, dead. . . ."

As we pick up the story, Binx has just awakened to the vague possibility of a search. What is a search? A search occurs when familiar objects and actions become clues that lead one to further encounters and further clues. His awakening launches Binx on a search to find his roots, his purpose, and his very identity.

Percy's novel—which earned him a National Book Award for fiction in 1962—unfolds during the last few days of Mardi Gras.

As New Orleans celebrates, Binx sets out on a semicomic yet deadly earnest hunt for meaning. We meet his stepfamily in their large house in the Garden District, along with his cousin Kate who, if anything, is more troubled than Binx. Suicidal and despairing, Kate needs his help, but his ever-threatening melancholy has left him powerless.

Binx looks for a "sign" that will certify he exists in the world. The sight of a black man coming from church on Ash Wednesday with a faint smudge on his forehead gives Binx both hope that signs are indeed given and the courage to be an anchor on which Kate can moor her fragile soul.

Walker Percy's life was its own kind of search for meaning. Orphaned at a young age by his father's suicide and his mother's accidental death, Percy was raised by an older cousin in an intellectual household. He was trained to be a doctor but the practice of medicine left him unsatisfied, so he turned to philosophy and then fiction. *The Moviegoer* made him famous.

In a 1983 interview he said that "the common thread that runs through all of my novels is of a man, or a woman, who finds himself/herself outside of society, maybe even in a state of neurosis, psychosis, or derangement. . . . What I try to do is always pose the question, Is this man or woman more abnormal than the 'normal society' around them?"

THE EDGE OF SADNESS

(1961 ✦ Fiction)

EDWIN O'CONNOR

(1918–1968)

Edwin O'Connor burst into public consciousness in 1956 with the publication of his second novel, *The Last Hurrah*, about a rascally politician making his final run at public office. The book, and later the film, was set in the Irish neighborhoods of New England—the once-ghetto neighborhoods that were moving into respectability after World War II, but still reeked of ethnic characters and traditions.

The Edge of Sadness mines the same territory and time period as that earlier novel but puts its institutional focus on the church rather than the political machine. Father Hugh Kennedy returns to his home diocese after "drying out" at a rehab clinic in the Southwest. He is still fragile from his struggle with alcoholism and content to take a parish in a run-down part of the city. He prefers to remain far from his former church where he disgraced himself. Inevitably, however, he is drawn into the circle of the Carmody family that he knew while growing up.

Charlie Carmody, his late father's best friend, is a character to equal Frank Skeffingston, the colorful ex-mayor of *The Last Hurrah*. "Old Charlie," as he calls himself, is the misogynist, manipulative, and thoroughly charming paterfamilias of the Carmodys. At least Father Hugh finds him charming; Charlie's own children have less kind feelings. One of his children is a daughter that Hugh might have married. Another is a priest who is now pastor of Hugh's old church.

The time period is the era just prior to Vatican II, when priests still wore birettas and prayed their breviaries. The mass was in Latin, all bishops were wise, and people looked up to their clergy who sometimes cracked under the pressure of the laity's adulation and expectation. No one, heaven knows, was in therapy or even in spiritual direction.

The Edge of Sadness is a long book. Perhaps O'Connor could have made it shorter, but the leisurely pace allows him to explore the prickly characters he clearly loves. There are hilarious conversations around the dinner table, even as a cloud of melancholy pervades the background. One of his more memorable characters is Father Danowski, the young Polish curate in Father Hugh's church. Danowski is pompous and naive, the eternal foil for Hugh's and Old Charlie's humor. Yet he is also goodhearted and energetic—the very image of a "good priest" of the church in that era.

Edwin O'Connor died prematurely in 1968. One wonders how he would have written about the post–Vatican II church. As it is, the world he chose to explore is fully realized, caught in midstride, preserved in amber.

The Edge of Sadness won the Pulitzer Prize for fiction in 1961.

MORTE D'URBAN

(1962 ✦ Fiction)

J. F. POWERS

(1917–1999)

Let us now praise Urban Roche, the golden-tongued preacher and well-connected fundraiser for the Order of St. Clement (a.k.a. the Clementines), the most spectacularly mediocre religious community in fact or fiction. Father Urban is a man who can talk his way around millionaires, who knows how the world is put together, and who likes to travel first class. Do the Clementines know what to do with a man of his caliber? Of course not.

Out of the blue Father Urban is transferred to an unsuccessful retreat house, more like a gulag, on the steppes of Minnesota where the popular preacher spends his time painting walls and sanding floors under the misdirection of Father Wilf Bestudik, his superior.

Not to worry. Father Urban is resourceful. Observing that the retreat house was failing to attract the better class of Catholic, he initiates a scheme to build a golf course on the property and finds a benefactor to underwrite it. Suddenly the combined spiritual retreat/golf weekend is drawing droves of laymen—not to mention clergy. Father Urban is riding high.

Of course that was before he was struck on the head by a golf ball hit by the bishop of Great Plains, and before the disastrous fishing weekend to Bloodsucker Lake. And by that time Father Urban had fallen out of favor with Mrs. Thwaites, the wealthy widow whose mansion has an elevator that can whisk her to a bomb shelter in the basement. And then there was that episode with Mrs. Thwaites's daughter, Sally. Well, better not go into that . . .

J. F. Powers has written a comic novel that truly plums the depths of its main character. Father Urban is an operator, to be sure, but underneath it all he cares about the state of people's souls. Chief among these is Billy Cosgrove, the millionaire whose generosity makes the golf course possible. Father Urban takes Billy's money but would also like to lead Billy along the path of Christian virtue. A delicate undertaking. Maybe, in the end, too delicate for Father Urban.

The humor in *Morte d'Urban* is as dry as a Minnesota winter. Powers never cracks a smile as he describes the escapades of Father Urban, the Clementines, and their rival religious communities, the Dalmations and Dolomites. Father Wilf's penny-pinching ways as superior of the retreat house are spelled out in ridiculously solemn detail. Father Urban's speech, which made such a splash at the annual Poinsettia Smorgasbord in the Greenwich Village Room of the General Diggles Hotel, is described in all its particulars—including the questions raised from the floor by Sylvia Bean whose "mind had been conditioned, if not impaired, by reading the Catholic press."

Morte d'Urban was awarded the 1963 National Book Award for fiction. It is part of a small body of work by J. F. Powers who wrote only two novels and three collections of short stories, nearly all of them set in the American Midwest. Powers was a pacifist who spent part of World War II in prison. He later taught at St. John's College (now St. John's University) in Collegeville, Minnesota.

JOURNAL OF A SOUL

(1964 ✦ Autobiography)

POPE JOHN XXIII

(1881–1963)

It really looks as if God has lavished upon me his most tender and motherly care . . . and through countless acts of kindness he has brought me here to Rome. It must be for some particular purpose of His." So writes Angelo Roncalli when he is twenty-one and a seminarian in Rome. The observation is remarkable not only because it attributes "motherly" qualities to God, but also because it shows Roncalli already suspects God may have something planned for him. In the same journal entry written in December of 1902 he continues, "Even if I were to be Pope, even if my name were to be invoked and revered by all and inscribed on marble monuments, I should still have to stand [in death] before the divine judge, and what would I be worth then? Not much."

These are clearly the reflections of a humble man. Think of them when you stand before his marble monument in St. Peter's Basilica. Remember them as you read his *Journal of a Soul*. Pope John XXIII became great by first becoming small. He worked at it, and this journal, written for the most part on retreats during the years of his training and ministry, records the effort. The journal was found after his death, some of it on loose pieces of paper folded and worn from frequent rereading. It appears that the pope wanted to learn and relearn the lessons of his own spiritual journey. By reading this journal, we can learn them as well.

The journal tracks Roncalli's career as secretary to the bishop of Bergamo, as a teacher and spiritual director at the Bergamo seminary, as a Vatican bureaucrat, and, in 1925, as a bishop and diplomat for the Holy See. He finds that his "many trials" in the diplomatic service most often have their origin in the Vatican itself, causing him to note ruefully, "This is a form of mortification and humiliation that I did not expect and which hurts me deeply."

The journal is not autobiographical in the sense that it tells the details of his life and the people he encountered. Big swaths of his life are missing. We hear nothing, for instance, of his service as a chaplain in the Italian army during World War I. Politicians, kings, and famous people are nowhere in sight. It is strictly a spiritual journal. Early entries, written during his youth, are excessively self-critical, as Roncalli struggles to get his impulsive nature in hand. Later, as an older man, he is more serene. He has won his self-control. Quoting Francis de Sales, he remarks, "I am like a bird singing in a thicket of thorns."

Roncalli trusted that his innate friendliness and charity would succeed better than political maneuvering, and he was right. As he observed during his time as a nuncio in Paris in 1947, "I leave to everyone else the superabundant cunning and so-called skill of the diplomat, and continue to be satisfied with my own *bonhomie* and simplicity of feeling, word and behaviour."

Tracking this *Journal of a Soul* is facilitated by the chronology of the pope's life that appears in the front of the book. The appendix includes the personal rule of ascetical practices that he followed all his life, and which turned him into a humble soul and a great man.

THE DOCUMENTS

(1966 ✦ Documentation)

VATICAN COUNCIL II
(1962–1965)

It is hard for younger Catholics today to imagine the Roman Catholic church before the Second Vatican Council. Suffice it to say the twenty-first-century church, for all of its problems, is a different world entirely. Gone are the cultural blinders Catholics hid behind to proclaim themselves the "one true church" possessing the "fullness of truth." Gone are the Latin rites with pointless multiplication of signs that mystified and marginalized the faithful. Gone is the Roman structure groaning under the weight of Europeans, the legalistic mind-sets, the rote conformity of parishes and religious communities.

Yet more reforming needs to be done in this post–Vatican II era. Forty years after the council, the church is still working out the ramifications of what the world's bishops debated in four council sessions. We need to read and reread their findings, to pray over them and experiment with them. The documents of Vatican II ought to be in every Catholic's library.

Consider the new ground that was broken in the sixteen documents (constitutions, decrees, and declarations) of Vatican II:

The Constitution on the Church reimagined the church primarily as a "people," not as an institutional structure. And these people of God were acknowledged to be pilgrims on the road to a promised land, rather than people who had already arrived.

The Constitution on the Sacred Liturgy not only opened the door to cultural adaptation of heretofore rigid worship services, it affirmed that church rites were not the sole property of clerics but belonged by right to the faithful as "full, conscious, and active" participants.

The Pastoral Constitution on the Church in the Modern World turned away from that old dichotomy of the "good church in an evil world." Instead, said the council, the world is a place where the Spirit is already mysteriously at work and where the faithful must "read the signs of the times" to understand their mission.

The Declaration on Religious Liberty jettisoned the age-old Catholic notion that "error has no rights" and affirmed instead that people have a right to their religious experience even if it differs from the Catholic one. Faced with the need to justify this new teaching in light of past statements, the council fathers gulped hard and confessed this was "a development of doctrine."

There are those who believe church leaders have attempted to undermine the work of the council in the years since it ended. Certainly there has been a negative reaction in some quarters, but the wish of Pope John XXIII to "let some air into the church" has been realized. It's too late now to shut the window. The church is committed.

In 2006 Pope Benedict XVI encouraged the editors of the Jesuit magazine *La Civiltà Cattolica* to let the teachings of the Second Vatican Council be its beacon, its "lighthouse," adding that the council's "doctrinal and pastoral riches" have not been fully appreciated.

The pope's admonition applies not merely to those editors but to all Catholics.

SILENCE

(1966 ◆ Fiction)

SHUSAKU ENDO

(1923–1996)

When Francis Xavier first brought Christianity to Japan in 1549, the Japanese islands were barely known to Westerners. It was a closed society, inimical to outsiders. While Xavier didn't stay, other Catholic missionaries who followed made a good beginning with the Japanese, introducing the Christian faith as well as new trade and scientific ideas. By the early seventeenth century about 300,000 Japanese had converted to Christianity.

Then things changed. Concerned about foreign influence, Japanese leaders first discouraged and then brutally persecuted Portuguese missionaries—mostly Jesuits—and those Japanese who had accepted baptism. Catholics were burned, drowned, or tortured until they denied their faith or died. This did not stop European missionaries from continuing to enter Japan secretly and minister to the persecuted Christian remnant.

This is the setting for Shusaku Endo's novel *Silence*, which he based on real people and events. Two young Portuguese Jesuits land at night on Kyushu, Japan's southernmost major island. They find refuge in a Christian fishing village but are forced to hide, living in squalor and fear. One of the missionaries, Sebastian Rodriguez, witnesses the martyrdom of two Japanese by drowning and writes in distress to his superiors about "the silence of God . . . the feeling that while men raise their voices in anguish God remains with folded arms, silent."

Rodriguez is a young man of high ideals. He accepts the fact of his eventual martyrdom, confident it will unite him more closely to the crucified Christ. He is determined to not apostatize—to save his life by denying his faith as some previous missionaries have done.

Separated from his companion, Rodriguez is eventually captured and subjected to intense psychological grilling. His captors plead with him to apostatize, promising to release Japanese Christians from punishment if he will deny his faith. Should he symbolically trample on the image of Christ and save his own life and others or be tortured and die? He imagines Christ telling him, "Trample! Trample! It is to be trampled on by you that I am here." In this quandary Rodriguez arrives at the supreme moment of his life.

Shusaku Endo converted to Catholicism with his mother when he was a child in Japan. He confessed later in life to be slightly ill at ease in his Christian skin, but it was too much a part of him to shuck off. In *Silence* his characters debate whether Japan can ever provide the soil for Christian evangelization. At one point, a missionary who has already apostatized complains to Rodriguez, "This country is a swamp. In time you will come to see that for yourself. . . . Whenever you plant a sapling in this swamp the roots begin to rot; the leaves grow yellow and wither. And we have planted the sampling of Christianity in this swamp."

Rodriquez is tormented by the notion that his Japanese converts may not have a clear understanding of the Christian God they are dying for. Such questions further confuse his moral dilemma. Taken together they make *Silence* a disturbing and memorable reading experience.

VATICAN COUNCIL II

(*1968* ✦ *History*)

XAVIER RYNNE

(*1914–2002*)

A few days after Pope John XXIII opened the Second Vatican
Council amid pomp and splendor in Rome, an article
appeared in *The New Yorker* titled "Letter from Vatican City." The
letter was a report on the council preparations. It was not a dry
summary of documents, but a vivid account of machinations
within the Roman curia, political maneuvering, how the battle for
the soul of the council was being joined, and who the players were.
Some in Rome were scandalized. They were so naive about press
coverage in those days that the American bishops didn't even have
a press officer.

This magazine piece, and the articles that followed, were signed
"Xavier Rynne"—a pseudonym. A few suspected, but couldn't
prove, that the author was really Francis X. Murphy, an American
Redemptorist priest then assigned to the Academy Alfonsiana in
Rome. He was also an advisor to an American bishop and, as such,
had access to inside information. Only years later did Murphy
acknowledge that he was indeed the author of the letters, but by
then the name Xavier Rynne had appeared on four books and was
indelibly connected to the council story.

Vatican Council II is a compilation of those letters and books
that so shocked the establishment in the 1960s, shining fresh light
on the once-hidden workings of the Vatican. It still makes compelling reading. The book offers a day-by-day unfolding of this
watershed event in the life of the church, telling what went on in
the council hall and in the coffeeshops and hallways behind the

scenes. Murphy admits he was "never one to shrink from politics at any level," and in his telling the Vatican is not much different from political wards of Boston or Chicago. Read forty years later the pieces lack historical perspective, but they more than make up for that with their wealth of gritty detail.

We read how Cardinal Liénart and Cardinal Frings stood up in the First General Congregation and challenged the makeup of council commissions stacked with curial favorites, insisting that they be more representative of the world's bishops. We share the amazement of the council fathers when Pope John in his opening address attacked "prophets of doom" in his own household. We shake our heads in disbelief when—during a debate over concelebration—a theologian warned the American bishops that if one hundred priests concelebrate one mass the church will wind up ninety-nine masses short.

Some recent critics of the book have labeled it a liberal rant from the older generation. It is certainly true that Rynne/Murphy wrote with an ideological slant. Many of his predictions about a radically changed church have not been realized in the period of reassessment after the council. None of that, however, changes the basic facts of what took place in Rome in the 1960s. And for a church that changes with agonizing slowness, the full impact of Vatican II may not be apparent for another century.

The existing volume combines four books in one, making it formidable to read. It would have benefited from a subject index as well as a name index. Still, the insider's account of what happened at Vatican Council II makes quite a story, and Xavier Rynne was perfectly placed to tell it.

THE GEOGRAPHY OF FAITH

(1971 ✦ Spirituality)

DANIEL BERRIGAN *(born 1921)* and
ROBERT COLES *(born 1929)*

In May of 1968, when the Vietnam War was at its height, nine persons, including Jesuit Daniel Berrigan and his brother Philip Berrigan, a Josephite priest, entered the draft board in Catonsville, Maryland, carried several hundred draft records into the parking lot outside, and set them afire. The nine surrendered to police, were tried and sentenced to varying terms in federal prison. When the time came to enter prison, though, some of them went into hiding as a further act of disobedience. Sheltered by friends, moving from house to house, Daniel Berrigan was not apprehended by federal agents until August of the following year.

During Berrigan's time in hiding, Harvard psychiatrist Robert Coles was approached by some friends about meeting the fugitive priest. Coles was initially wary. Although he, too, was against the war, Coles preferred different forms of protest. At last he relented, met Berrigan, and the two had several taped conversations that were later published as *The Geography of Faith*, a classic of Christian activism.

At first in their discussions Coles is a polite listener and questioner. Berrigan keeps boring in on him, suggesting that academic answers were not enough: the times demand that people put their lives on the line. Says Berrigan, "I am trying to live now . . . in a way that points to the future and indicates the directions I believe we must all take. . . . The fate of people, of the world, demand[s] that one not be merely a listener, or a good friend, but yes, be in trouble."

At one point Berrigan asks him why there are no psychiatrists in jail at this moment in history, a question that Coles never satisfactorily answers.

Finally Coles, who would later win a Pulitzer Prize for his writing on children in crisis, is moved to abandon his therapeutic reserve. His biographer, Bruce Ronda, later described it as a "watershed experience" for Coles.

Coles is a believer but not a churchgoer. He accepts Berrigan's distinction between personal piety and the kind of faith that embraces social reform. He confesses,

> "People like me spend a lot of time discussing the violence of the radical left, and at the same time—because of the kind of lives we live, because of the comforts and privileges we enjoy— do not dare to look at the institutionalized violence that is sometimes masked and veiled but is part of everyday life."

There are parts of *The Geography of Faith* that are dated, with frequent reference to the Black Panthers, the Weathermen, and school integration in the South, all of which dominated the news in those days. Berrigan is the more romantic of the two. He believes the younger generation is leading the way to permanent social change. (This is before the younger generation voted *en masse* for Ronald Reagan.) Coles is less optimistic about the future.

Yet *The Geography of Faith* is still compelling reading, since there is no less need for prophetic leadership in our own day. With Berrigan and Coles we can be strengthened by knowing—as Berrigan put it— that Christ, at the hour of his death, "declared so explicitly his own solidarity with . . . the tradition of the outsider, the dissenter, the critic who dares to speak the extremely upsetting and painful truth."

CHRISTIAN ZEN

(1971 ◆ *Spirituality*)

WILLIAM JOHNSTON
(*born 1925*)

Words are like a finger pointing to the moon.
Grab hold of the finger, and you cannot see the moon.

—Zen saying

There are two "ways" of prayer in the Christian tradition, and in religion generally—the cataphatic and the apophatic. The cataphatic uses what we know about God as grist for prayer, for instance by praying with scripture or meditating on the passion of Christ. The apophatic way, exemplified by John Cassian and *The Cloud of Unknowing*, weighs God's ultimate unknowability and advocates wordless (even idealess) prayer.

The Buddhist Zen practice is emphatically apophatic. People sit for long periods of time in silent meditation, making every effort to empty their minds, since thoughts, if they do come, are not God.

William Johnston is an Irish Jesuit stationed at Sophia University in Tokyo where after Vatican II he got involved in the Christian-Buddhist dialogue and ultimately became a Zen practitioner. He believes that using Zen as a mode of Christian prayer could get Christianity out of its conceptual rut and push Christians to use more of their psychic muscle. After sitting *zazen* for some time he has discerned a certain laziness in Western approaches to prayer.

There are, of course, challenges for Christians using Zen meditation. For one, Buddhists are opposed to any kind of dualism, whether it is God/human or body/soul. They insist cheerfully that "all is one," which is fine except that it makes dialogue about theology almost impossible. Then there is the Christological problem. Christian prayer—even the wordless kind—is always directed in and through Christ. Johnston believes Christians must always insist on this point, but he also believes that even here we have something to learn from Zen. Zen, he says, can help us separate our "words about Christ" from Christ himself. Like the finger/moon analogy in the saying above, we must focus on the reality, not the finger that points.

The opening chapters of *Christian Zen* recount Johnston's early experiences with East-West dialogue. The middle chapters consider the similarities and differences of Buddhist and Christian Zen, and the final portion of the book offers practical suggestions for experiencing Zen as Christian prayer and the task of achieving enlightenment.

Christian Zen is not a great book in the sense that it explores Zen or Christian asceticism in a deep way. It is short and serves more as an introduction than a definitive treatment. Johnston writes in a chatty, familiar style and is not above poking fun at Ireland or California along the way. His book, however, is significant in ways that Johnston himself is aware of. Since the first publication of the book in 1970 the church in Asia has grown enormously, especially in Korea, the Philippines, South India, and Sri Lanka. The East is going to impact the global church in major ways still unknown. *Christian Zen* is an important first word.

THE WOUNDED HEALER

(*1972* ✦ *Spirituality*)

HENRI NOUWEN

(1932–1996)

The last decades of the twentieth century witnessed a growing emphasis on church ministry. After the Second Vatican Council the glow was gone from "filling station" parishes where people lined up to receive the sacraments and "get grace." Now Catholics wanted a more intimate connection with their parish. In addition, the decline in the number of priests and the appearance of lay ministers shifted emphasis from the ritual priesthood to ministry broadly conceived. Suddenly everyone was a minister.

The most influential voice in the formation of ministers during this era was Henri Nouwen, a Dutch-born Catholic priest who taught successively at Notre Dame, Yale, and Harvard. Nouwen was revered by his students, both Catholic and Protestant. He published a score of books on prayer and ministry, including *Creative Ministry, Reaching Out*—and his paradigmatic work, *The Wounded Healer.*

Nouwen, whose teaching was focused on ministers in training, laments in that book how poorly prepared most ministers are when invited to be spiritual leaders. "I am afraid," he writes, "that in a few decades the church will be accused of having failed in its most basic task: to offer men [and women] creative ways to communicate with the sources of human life."

Most ministers assume that when confronted with a person in need they must be strong, self-assured, and have all the answers. Just the opposite is true, according to Nouwen. Truly effective ministers are in touch with their own failings and not afraid to share them with a wounded world. "As soon as we feel at home in our own house, discover the dark corners as well as the light spots, the closed doors as well as the drafty rooms, our confusion will evaporate, our anxiety will diminish, and we will become capable of creative work," he writes.

Nouwen believes one's personal wounds are not barriers to ministry—they are doors. They create a common ground for those who are hurting and in need of comfort. The minister, says Nouwen, must tend to the core of his or her own self and be comfortable there, adding, "When we have found the anchor places for our lives in our own center, we can be free to let others enter into the space created for them and allow them to dance their own dance, sing their own song and speak their own language without fear."

Henri Nouwen lived what he preached. In person he was mercurial, sensitive, prone to fits of angst and bouts of depression, but also endlessly empathetic. His writing is marked by spiritual delicacy and depth of feeling. If this book is sometimes dated in the examples it uses, his conclusions are timeless and still capable of moving us.

The idea of "the wounded healer" became a catchphrase in religious circles during Nouwen's lifetime. He insisted that he was advocating more than just a ministerial technique. It was a life stance. As he wrote, "Making one's own wounds a source of healing . . . does not call for a sharing of superficial personal pains but for a constant willingness to see one's own pain and suffering as rising from the depth of the human condition which all men share."

MODELS OF THE CHURCH

(1974 ◆ Theology)

AVERY DULLES
(born 1918)

In no area did Vatican Council II carve out more new ground than with its theology of church. While liturgical reforms had a more immediate effect, these represented a return to earlier forms of worship. The council's theology of church (or ecclesiology, to use the technical term) was something new altogether. Its definition of the church as "the people of God," while compelling, left both church professionals and the faithful struggling to fit into a new identity.

The publication of *Models of the Church* less than a decade later took the pressure off by proposing alternative ways the institution and its people could view themselves. It was like finally having a closet full of clothes after wearing one outfit for months on end. The book by Jesuit theologian Avery Dulles was snatched up by seminary and university classes and by lay formation programs. In theological circles, it was a phenomenon.

Dulles offers five different images of church. His "models" are not metaphors exactly or scaled-down reproductions. Rather, each of them views the church under an aspect that simultaneously illuminates and limits its mysterious reality. The illumination and the limitation are equally telling. In brief, he says we can envision:

The Church as Institution. On one hand, the church must be an institution, but this view would make the institutional element primary. Its strength comes from making the church visible, its weakness from putting obedience above other virtues or using theology just to defend official positions. It finds very little basis in scripture.

The Church as Mystical Communion. Here the church is more of a brotherhood than an institution. This is a more scriptural image, evoking Paul's vine and branches, the Mystical Body of Christ, and the people of God. But, says Dulles, the image risks "unhealthy divinization," and, he asks, "How can any particular group [of people] claim that they, and they alone, are God's people?"

The Church as Sacrament. This describes church as a sign—as an actual event—of God's grace in the world. Vatican II proclaimed the church as sacrament. However, in Dulles's view, " . . . sacramentalism, carried to excess, can induce an attitude of narcissistic aestheticism that is not easily reconcilable with a full Christian commitment to social and ethical values."

The Church as Herald. This image gives emphasis to the church's role in proclaiming the word. Popular among Protestants, it can empower the church to mission. On the other hand, Catholics tend to stress the incarnational word: the word made flesh. And the herald image runs the risk of stressing witness at the expense of social action, says Dulles.

The Church as Servant. This is the "secular-dialogic" image central to the council's Pastoral Constitution on the Church in the Modern World. Under this sign doctrine and sacramentalism are subordinated to social engagement. While it has a strong basis in scripture, the church adopting this model may compromise its role of prophetic opposition to the world's values.

Avery Dulles maintains that no one of these models, taken alone, really satisfies. The community of disciples that is the church must borrow from each of them, and in so doing it must know the risks of borrowing.

PILGRIM AT TINKER CREEK

(1974 ✦ Spirituality)

ANNIE DILLARD

(born 1945)

S eeking God in the world of nature is as old as humans themselves. Even in prehistoric times people were awed by watching the heavens and found wonder in the fecundity of earth.

As a source of revelation, however, nature has a mixed message:
It deals in death as well as life, hurricanes as well as April showers.
The snow-capped mountains, so lovely to behold, are the end
products of blind tectonic forces, earthquakes, and cataclysms.

As people of faith, should we, then, be comforted by nature or
appalled by its cold, cold heart? This is the question that runs
through Annie Dillard's Pulitzer Prize–winning book, *Pilgrim at
Tinker Creek*. Dillard describes a year spent living in a cabin by a
creek in the Shenandoah Valley of Virginia. Birds come and go with
the seasons. Greenery bursts forth in the spring to be munched all
summer by insects and animals. Praying mantises hatch from egg
cases outside her window and go forth to eat other insects and each
other. Nature is not always pretty on close inspection.

The central image in Dillard's book is the creek itself that carries water down from the Blue Ridge Mountains, past Dillard's
door, and then to the sea. It gathers and scatters. With the author,
we sit on its banks and learn to live in the moment. She writes,

"My God, I look at the creek. It is the answer to Merton's
prayer, 'Give us time!' It never stops. If I seek the senses and
skill of children, the information of a thousand books, the
innocence of puppies, even the insights of my own city past, I

do so only, solely, and entirely that I may look well at the creek. You don't run down the present, pursue it with baited hooks and nets. You wait for it, empty handed, and you are filled. You'll have fish left over. The creek is the one great giver. It is, by definition, Christmas, the incarnation. This old rock planet gets the present for a present on its birthday every day."

During the summer months Dillard watches muskrats and discovers how to empty herself and become part of the landscape lest the muskrats stay in hiding. She compares this to the study of subatomic particles by physicists and how their certainty coexists with uncertainty: "The electron is a muskrat; it cannot be perfectly stalked. . . . It is not that we lack sufficient information to know both a particle's velocity and its position. . . . Rather, we know for sure that there is no knowing."

The world of nature is grace, is mystery, is known and yet unknown. In the twenty-fifth anniversary edition of *Pilgrim at Tinker Creek* Dillard added an afterword in which she confesses she set out to write a theodicy—an argument for God's goodness in spite of the presence of pain and darkness. The first half of the book describes the positive route to God, through knowledge of God's attributes; the second half plumbs God's mystery and unknowability.

Pilgrim at Tinker Creek is a wondrous book, to be read for sheer pleasure even if one doesn't follow every turn of the argument. In the end you may agree with Annie Dillard that the universe "was not made in jest but in solemn incomprehensible earnest," but you will also experience joy and give thanks for it.

LAMY OF SANTA FE

(1975 ◆ Biography)

PAUL HORGAN

(1903–1995)

Willa Cather's classic novel *Death Comes for the Archbishop* tells the story of Jean Marie Latour, who came to the Southwest as apostolic administrator of Santa Fe and labored there for decades to build the church. As it turns out, Cather's story was built on a real-life person who later became the subject of a Pulitzer Prize–winning biography by Paul Horgan.

His real name was Jean Baptist Lamy, and *Lamy of Santa Fe* tells a story no less colorful than Cather's. Along the way, it provides a history of the American Southwest at a crucial time in its development. Absorbed into the United States as a result of the Mexican War in the 1840s, the New Mexico Territory had no roads, no schools, and no enduring institutions other than the Catholic church—and that once-proud creation of Franciscan missionaries was nearly in ruin.

Jean Baptist Lamy was raised and ordained in France. Recruited to be a missionary in Ohio, he served there for eleven years, preaching, building churches, and administering the sacraments. Modest and hardworking, Lamy was astonished when he was suddenly named a bishop and appointed to Santa Fe. He was accompanied by Joseph Machebeuf, his friend since their seminary days in France.

Santa Fe at that time was a wild place. Just getting there was a problem. The new bishop took a boat down the Ohio and Mississippi rivers to New Orleans, then a steamboat to Galveston and Indianola, Texas. At the last port the steamer was wrecked and

Lamy lost most of his possessions. In Texas he joined an army caravan to El Paso, then turned north into New Mexico and on to Santa Fe—in all, a modest trip of 2,200 miles.

In those days the New Mexico Territory had a land area larger than France, comprising the present states of New Mexico, Arizona, Colorado, and parts of Texas. Lamy calculated it had 68,000 Catholics, twenty-six churches (most of them falling apart), and twelve native priests who wouldn't obey Lamy because they felt they still owed obedience to the Mexican bishop of Durango. It took years to get the jurisdiction issue sorted out, and years to create an effective clergy and working Catholic institutions in the territory.

Paul Horgan, who won a previous Pulitzer for his history of the Rio Grande, has an eye for the land and the customs of the Southwest. He knows how to describe nights under the stars as Lamy and Machebeuf ride to distant mission outposts. He is also good at capturing the friendship between the two men who grow old together, who are so different in temperament and yet are moved by the same ideals and faith. Machebeuf eventually became the first bishop of Denver.

Many Catholic biographies of old heaped such adoring praise on their subjects that the books became suspect, a source of piety rather than information. Under Paul Horgan's sure hand, *Lamy of Santa Fe* is historically sound and yet a deeply human story of an earnest and admirable man.

RETURN TO THE CENTER

(1976 ◆ Spirituality)

BEDE GRIFFITHS

(1906–1993)

In his book *The Golden String*, Bede Griffiths described his transformation from skeptical schoolboy to believer during his student years at Oxford. Subsequently he became a Roman Catholic and then a Benedictine monk. C. S. Lewis, his college tutor, had a significant role in that first story.

Now skip ahead some forty years. Griffiths is still a Benedictine but is no longer in Britain. He is bearded, walks barefoot, wears the robes of a Hindu holy man, and lives in a rude hut in Shantivanam ashram near the southern tip of India. One may wonder what path he has been following. In *Return to the Center* he tells us—not the details of the journey but the fascinating landscape in which he now finds himself.

Needless to say, the "center" Griffiths writes about is not the center described in the language of traditional Catholic theology. It is the center beyond theology, beyond words or symbols, beyond thinking. In the years since 1955 when he first went to India, he learned from Eastern religions and found present in all religions "one Truth . . . which cannot properly be expressed in words but has to be realized within." Without leaving Catholicism, he is able to affirm that all religions are striving for "the one unchanging Light reflecting itself in human consciousness."

Return to the Center is not proposing a new, amalgamated religion. Griffiths is a Christian. However he has come to see his faith from a new vantage point that both highlights its strengths and deepens its mystery. In a series of brief chapters he proposes a metaphysical grounding for all religions that, along the way, helps to illuminate traditional Catholic doctrine. He writes: "The Fall is the fall into self-consciousness"; "Sin is the failure to realize the self"; "Redemption . . . is the return to unity" that was fragmented by sin. Read in context, Griffiths's observations keep exploding from the pages.

Griffiths holds a Platonic view of the structure of reality. The world of God is the real one, he says, while the world we see is only a shadow of God's world. He is dismissive of science and technology—mere sense experiences, in his view, that distract us from going deeply into our selves.

Return to the Center is a work of profound spirituality rather than nuanced theology. If one can quibble now and then with Griffiths's formulations, one cannot help but be impressed by his sincerity. This is a man who has lived his beliefs, who has walked the path, who has integrated his faith, and who speaks from experience. We should all live such an interesting life. So we are buoyed when we hear him say,

"Each man must therefore discover this Center in himself, this Ground of his being, this Law of his life. It is hidden in the depths of every soul, waiting to be discovered. It is the treasure hidden in the field, the pearl of great price. It is the one thing which is necessary, which can satisfy all our desires and answer all our needs."

THE GREAT MYSTERIES

(1976 ✦ Spirituality)

ANDREW M. GREELEY

(born 1928)

The long period of Catholic retrenchment under Pope John Paul II and Pope Benedict XVI has emphasized doctrinal correctness and the church's obligation to proclaim the truth of Christianity. As one prelate in the Midwest was quoted as saying, "There are objective truths. There is right and wrong. Holy Mother Church is our mother who loves us, and she knows best."

Such words reflect a long and honorable tradition. Unfortunately, however, they suggest an image of the Vatican and the bishops presiding over a lockbox of truths from which are doled out crumbs to the waiting faithful. It is a lockbox that grows ever larger as the years go by. One need only compare the ancient Nicene Creed (173 Latin words) to the contemporary *Catechism of the Catholic Church* (848 pages).

There is another way of coming at the central reality of Christianity. Instead of seeing it as series of connected "truths," one can evoke it as a series of connected mysteries. "Mystery" is a softer word, to be sure—without the bite of "truth," but also without the arrogance. A mystery is open-ended and allows the believer to enter in. What's more, mysteries are located not in some external lockbox but in our own humanity. Here we find the mystery of God intertwined with our own.

Andrew Greeley has taken this second way in *The Great Mysteries*, a book that anchors Christian faith deep in human life. He begins by reflecting on the "something else" of life that so many people desire. He observes, "The most basic of religious questions—

maybe the only one that really matters—is whether we can accept the claim to graciousness and loving care that the Something Else seems to be making in our occasional encounters with it."

Then Greeley poses twelve questions that he identifies with the central mysteries of Christianity. Greeley asks, for instance, "Is it safe to trust?" then reflects on the mystery of the Holy Spirit that urges us to be open to the world, risking wounds and embarrassment. He asks, "Can guilt be wiped away?" then talks about the mystery of grace that overlooks and forgives our faults because God is first and last a lover, and that is what lovers do.

Greeley calls his book a "catechism" because it summarizes the central mysteries of Christianity—God, Jesus, the cross and resurrection, salvation, eucharist, the church, baptism, Mary, and heaven, among others. It is not like traditional catechisms, but that is the point. He often ends his chapters with doctrinal notes that deepen the connection with traditional teaching.

Andrew Greeley brings his own particular strengths to this undertaking. A novelist and storyteller, the Chicago priest is a trained (and working) sociologist who has always been particularly sensitive to the moods and hopes of American Catholics and who has never been afraid to stand with them.

He is also gifted with words. In his commentary on baptism, Greeley observes, "The world is a chalice of grace." Then he adds,

> "But the world is not a passive sacrament; the environment does not stand idly by waiting for us to perceive its graciousness. The Holy Spirit . . . is actively pursuing us with a world that commands our attention with its splendors and invites our admiration with its beauty.
>
> And grace is not merely lurking around the corner waiting for us; it is chasing us madly down the street."

A GUIDE FOR
THE PERPLEXED

(1977 ♦ Philosophy)

E. F. SCHUMACHER
(1911–1977)

Readers of a certain age will remember the economist and engineer Ernst Friedrich Schumacher as the author of *Small Is Beautiful*, a book of economic theory based on the proposition that "people matter." Schumacher, who was born in Germany but fled to England before World War II, wrote that 1973 book because he was convinced that neither socialism (state control of the economy) nor capitalism (control by bankers and industrialists) served the good of the people. Schumacher followed the lead of the British "distributists"—G. K. Chesterton, Hillaire Belloc, Eric Gill, and Dorothy L. Sayers—who believed that individuals and small businesses were best situated to direct the economy along humane lines.

Schumacher had become a Catholic while he was writing *Small Is Beautiful.* Not many people knew it. He had been contemplating the move for some years because he had found much wisdom in Catholic thinkers, including Dante and Thomas Aquinas. His encounter with the papal social encyclicals *Rerum Novarum* and *Quadragesimo Anno* left him "completely staggered," remarking, "Here were these celibates living in an ivory tower. . . . Why can they talk a great deal of sense when everyone else talks nonsense . . . ?"

In the wake of worldwide acclaim for *Small Is Beautiful,* Schumacher turned to what he called his "religious book," *A Guide for the Perplexed.* He borrowed the title from a twelfth-century work by Moses Maimonides, a Talmudic scholar who sought to reconcile religious faith and Aristotelian philosophy. This is Schumacher's aim as well. Modern science, he says, as with modern economics, deals only with surfaces: a grazing steer is seen only as meat, a factory machinist is only a unit of labor. In contrast, Schumacher stressed "the inwardness of things": farm animals possess mysterious life; the machinist has consciousness. He goes on to say, "Anything that we can destroy but are unable to make is, in a sense, sacred, and all our 'explanations' of it do not explain anything." Things and people have meaning only in their transcendent dimension that cannot be grasped by science or manipulated by governments. The real problems of life, he says, cannot be solved; they must be grappled with and ultimately transcended.

In the first three chapters of the book, Schumacher outlines the hierarchical nature of reality, and how the outward layers of reality presume the inner. Then he draws attention to our powers of perception, which always must be adequate for the sort of information desired. A man's spiritual well-being, for instance, cannot be measured by a sonogram. Finally, Schumacher describes the "four fields of knowledge" needed to comprehend reality in its wholeness. Using all of these we can seek our true "end" without fear of getting stuck at one of the steps along the way.

A Guide for the Perplexed is an intense, passionate, and closely argued book. It is not for casual reading. In a sense, it is a classical apologetic, a philosophical debate about the meaning of life. The fact that E. F. Schumacher is a thoroughly modern man addressing a thoroughly modern situation gives his book urgency and freshness.

SADHANA

(1978 ◆ Spirituality)

ANTHONY DE MELLO

(1931–1987)

Jesuit Anthony de Mello enjoyed great popularity in the 1970s and 1980s through his workshops and the books he wrote. De Mello had a buoyant manner and teaching skills honed by years as a retreat director in India. His Indian heritage also gave him a point of view useful for exposing Western rationality. He loved to tell stories that could bring listeners to a standstill—like the one of a fictional Master telling a disciple, "A thought is a screen, not a mirror; that is why you live in a thought-envelope, untouched by Reality."

Anthony de Mello died suddenly of a heart attack in 1987. A decade later a Vatican statement claimed that some of his later writings had distanced themselves from Christian teaching and were "incompatible with Catholic faith." Those critical of de Mello hailed it as a condemnation; the Vatican, though, had carefully avoided the c-word. Still, even some of de Mello's friends called him a pioneer in "post-denominational Christianity."

Sadhana: A Way to God was the first book de Mello published and the one that won him a great following. It gathers together many of the prayer and meditation techniques he developed for retreats. The Indian influence is evident, but the Christian content is paramount. He calls these "Christian exercises in Eastern form."

Sadhana contains forty-seven exercises to awaken prayer, leading to contemplation. De Mello believed that the most urgent need of believers was to become aware—of their bodies, their breath, their thoughts, and of silence itself. (This is a theme he returned to in a book published posthumously, *Awareness: The Perils and Opportunities of Reality*.) Once aware, people can better discern the presence of God, the touch of God, and the fact that God is also present in others.

A typical exercise in *Sadhana* focuses on the awareness of sounds. He tells people in his group to close their eyes, put their hands over their ears, and be attentive only to their breathing for ten breaths. Then, returning their hands to their laps, they listen carefully to each sound they hear, identifying and embracing it. This and similar exercises enrich our appreciation for life in all its variety and lead to acts of gratitude and praise.

In the second half of *Sadhana* de Mello uses the imagination to initiate prayer. Fantasy and imagination have a long tradition in Ignatian prayer. The book suggests imaginary landscapes and scenarios to dwell in attentively. The exercises are designed to bring us to choose among possible actions, allowing us to reflect on instinctive reactions and the deeper calls of God. There are also exercises to foster devotion in prayer.

Sadhana is a most useful book for individuals and groups. In his usual positive way, Anthony de Mello promises that these exercises, if faithfully practiced, will enhance one's sense of peace and joy. They are eminently practical and deeply spiritual.

CATHOLICISM

(1980 ✦ Theology)

RICHARD P. MCBRIEN

(born 1936)

Catholics have long cherished the notion that theirs is a distinctive vocation. Being a Catholic—being a part of the "Catholic thing," whatever that amounts to—puts them in a class by themselves. But what, precisely, makes Catholicism special? In the twentieth century this special quality was articulated by Karl Adam in *The Spirit of Catholicism*, mentioned earlier, and later by the distinguished French theologian Henri de Lubac, whose *Catholicism* was published in 1947.

In 1980 American theologian Richard McBrien at Notre Dame University set out to restate the distinctive qualities of the Catholic faith in the wake of the Second Vatican Council. He announced that his book would be "a bridge between the church of yesterday and the church of today, between conservative, traditionally minded Catholics, on one hand, and progressive, renewal-minded Catholics, on the other . . ."

In the twenty-five years since then, McBrien's *Catholicism* has established itself as a basic text on the Catholic faith in high schools and universities and as a reference work for general use. It was the most comprehensive narrative summary of Catholic belief in the years after the council.

Inevitably, after the first edition appeared questions were raised about McBrien's treatment of some topics, among them grace, contraception, Mary's virginity, the origins of the church, and the ordination of women. These were not allegations of error but issues that some felt needed clarification. Changes were made in the second

(1986) edition. A more substantial reorganization was undertaken in the third (1994) edition. The treatment of Mary was moved from the "Church" section and put in "Spirituality"; material was added covering new movements such as liberation theology; "Morality" and "Spirituality" became major independent sections.

This latest edition of *Catholicism* has seven parts: I. Human Existence (including nature, grace, original sin); II. God (belief and unbelief, the Trinity); III. Jesus Christ; IV. The Church; V. The Sacraments; VI. Christian Morality; VII. Christian Spirituality.

The volume concludes with a summary synthesis of Catholic belief. McBrien declares that the Petrine office is one distinctive feature of Catholicism. Even more, he says, it is the way the qualities of sacramentality, mediation, and community are configured that makes the Catholic faith truly special. According to McBrien, Catholicism is an inclusive faith that blends many streams in one. The big tent. Not "either/or," but "both/and."

So what is Catholicism? McBrien points out that "Catholic" is as much an adjective as a noun. It is a state of being. He says, "Catholicism is an understanding, affirmation and expression of human existence before it is a corporate conviction about the pope, or the seven sacraments, or even about Jesus Christ and redemption." To be Catholic is to be in a certain way.

It remains to be seen whether McBrien's *Catholicism* will be as influential in the years ahead as it was in the recent past. His big-tent faith and his wish to incorporate "both/and" may prove unwelcome to a church leadership that tries to define faith more narrowly. But even if that were so, that would not diminish the considerable achievement of Richard McBrien and his truly catholic survey of Catholicism.

AFTER VIRTUE

(1981 ✦ Moral Philosophy)

ALASDAIR MACINTYRE

(born 1929)

American politicians—perhaps politicians everywhere—like to say their policies are simply matters of putting right ahead of wrong. In our day, though, matters of right and wrong are rarely simple. Not only are issues such as war and abortion complex in themselves, but there is no consensus about ways to organize a public dialogue to resolve them. Different groups and individuals operate out of different premises.

Alasdair MacIntyre has done more than any other person in the last quarter-century to energize debate about the dilemmas of ethical decision making in daily living. His book *After Virtue* has been much discussed in academia and has influenced the movement of "virtue ethics" as a way of making value choices.

MacIntyre, who was born in Scotland and is presently a senior research professor of philosophy at Notre Dame, blames much of the ethical confusion today on the Enlightenment, which attempted to make human reason the basis for philosophy. The trouble is, this made philosophical truth dependent on the human doing the reasoning. Truth lost its connection with objective criteria and became a personal statement, and one person's truth was as good as another's. In MacIntyre's view this had a disastrous effect on ethical reasoning. He refers to it as "emotovism"—which, he says, is "the doctrine that all evaluative judgments are *nothing but* expressions of preference, expressions of attitude or feeling . . ."

It took MacIntyre some time to arrive at this position. He began as a Marxist but grew disillusioned when it became apparent that Marxism was not serving its stated goal of liberating the masses. He then moved toward Aristotelian ethics, which is built around virtues (i.e., habits) of good behavior. Within this system, the "good" being sought always stands in relation to the highest good, since unless there is a highest good to serve as a polestar, our choices of lesser goods will be aimless and disoriented.

For MacIntyre this highest good is God, but he is willing to concede that for nonbelievers tradition provides ample models for good behavior today just as it did for the ancient Greeks. Thus he represents a position close to the Catholic "natural law" position that posits the existence of objective standards of right and wrong accessible to all.

Indeed, according to *After Virtue*, we come to grasp the virtues of good behavior not as revealed truths but as observed practices. We watch the truly wise people in society and do as they do. Their lives teach us; their practices become our virtues.

Because MacIntyre writes historical rather than technical philosophy, *After Virtue* is accessible to nonspecialists. Still, it is a book for serious readers.

By the end of it MacIntyre confesses that he is not entirely sure the West has enough truly wise people to instruct all of us in virtue. He compares the present world to the era of the dissolution of the Roman Empire and warns of "the new dark ages which are already upon us." Perhaps what we need to do, he says, is "construct . . . local forms of community within which civility and the intellectual and moral life can be sustained. . . ." So what we really need is not another politician, but another St. Benedict.

WORD INTO SILENCE

(1981 ✦ Spirituality)

JOHN MAIN

(1926–1982)

John Main was a Benedictine instrumental in spreading the practice of meditation among Christians in many parts of the world.
Originally Main was trained in the law and went to the East as a
member of the British Colonial Service. In India he encountered a
Hindu meditation teacher, and this experience totally transformed
his life. Returning to England, Main joined the Benedictines at
Ealing Abbey, hoping to continue his meditation practice. His superiors told him to stop using a mantra on the grounds that it wasn't
in the Benedictine tradition—until he found a reference to it in the
writings of John Cassian and so was allowed to continue.

Main had the dream of creating communities built on meditation practice. With this in mind, he went to Canada in 1977,
and there founded the Benedictine Priory of Montreal where an
ecumenical group of clergy and laypeople was formed and where
it still continues. Today there are groups inspired by Main in many
countries. (The World Community for Christian Meditation, the
organization that he started, is headquartered in Britain.)

Word into Silence, John Main's most enduring book, is a short
work written with his distinctive clarity and grace. He announces
at the outset that "there is no greater need in the Church and in
the world today than for the renewed understanding that the call
to prayer, to deep prayer, is universal. Unity among Christians as
well as, in the long term, unity among different races and creeds
rests upon finding the inner principle of unity as a personal experience in our own hearts."

The statement reflects the unique quality of Main's vision. He sees meditation as a personal experience but also as a means to bridge cultures and bring people together, particularly people from the East and West.

Yet, while Main borrows language from the East, the aim of his meditation is indisputably Christian. "In meditation," he says, "we seek to enter as fully as we can into the now, and in entering into the now to live as fully as possible with the now-risen and ever-living Lord Jesus."

Word into Silence offers instruction on how to meditate. Even more, it offers a theological understanding of what is going on when we meditate. Main offers commentaries on New Testament texts that have a particular application to prayer experiences. He closes with an admonition to "set your mind on the Kingdom" and make it the center of daily living, finding fulfillment in the here and now.

One may wonder what the difference is between Main's style of meditation and the equally popular centering prayer propagated by Thomas Keating. Essentially there is none. However, Main tends to emphasize the communal fruits of prayer, and is more insistent on the use of the mantra to focus prayer. The mantra, he says, "is like a harmonic that we sound in the depths of our spirit, bringing us to an ever-deepening sense of our wholeness and central harmony."

PRIMARY SPEECH

(1982 ✦ Spirituality)

ANN BELFORD ULANOV *(born 1938)* and
BARRY ULANOV *(1918–2000)*

Prayer works two ways, stretching up (or out) to God while also stretching the humanity of those who pray, sifting and testing their assumptions, their honesty, and their very selves. For Ann and Barry Ulanov prayer is a kind of primary speech in which we fumble to say who God is and who we are. "To pray," they say, "is to listen to and hear this self who is speaking. This speech is primary because it is basic and fundamental, our ground. In prayer we say who in fact we are—not who we should be, or who we wish we were, but who we are. All prayer begins with this confession."

The Ulanovs, wife and husband, are uniquely qualified to come at prayer this way. Ann Belford Ulanov, an Episcopalian, is professor of psychiatry and religion at Union Theological Seminary. Barry Ulanov, a Catholic, was professor of English at Barnard College who also taught religion at Columbia University and Union Theological. A man of many talents, he was also a noted jazz critic and music producer, and an expert on early Christian art.

Their book is grounded in the belief that prayer—contrary to its popular image—is not an ethereal activity that takes place on some exalted plane of being. Real prayer is gritty and incarnational. It grows out of flesh-and-blood existence. It incorporates our day-to-day experiences whether we reflect on those experiences or not. In fact, sometimes we have to listen to our prayer to find out what's really going on.

After stating their thesis in chapter one, subsequent sections of the book take up various aspects of prayer: prayer and desire, prayer and its projected images of God, prayer and fantasy, prayer and fear, prayer and aggression, prayer and sexuality. Each section examines how these aspects of humanity color our prayer, to enrich it or sometimes to distort it. One can readily understand how childhood experiences affect our adult image of a parental God. The fact that such baggage gets dragged into prayer does not make prayer less authentic, however. We must pray from where we are.

Take sexuality, for example. Those of a Jansenistic persuasion would exclude sexuality from prayer. Not the Ulanovs. After pointing out how erotic images lend power to the *Song of Songs* and writings of the mystics, they urge us to borrow from our sexuality to enliven the way we pray. "We must bring to prayer the excitements, the wonders, the confusion, and the bruises that make up our lives in this area," they write. And, "Our life of desire prepares us for our life of prayer." It gives us a language and context for spiritual union with God.

The Ulanovs make the essential point that prayer is about otherness. When we pray, we pray to the Other. The relationship we establish with God inevitably touches all other relationships as well. As we pray with and for others, we are gently and gradually drawn into the community of a Trinitarian God.

According to Ann and Barry Ulanov, "Prayer tugs at us, pulls us into a life of . . . unceasing abundance. We become increasingly swept into the flowing of this other life through the small space of our self."

WE DRINK FROM OUR OWN WELLS

(1983 ✦ Spirituality)

GUSTAVO GUTIÉRREZ

(born 1928)

G ustavo Gutiérrez has been the leading exponent of liberation theology, which finds its origin in the efforts of poor and oppressed people in Latin America to secure economic and social justice. A Peruvian who now teaches at Notre Dame, Gutiérrez is best known for *A Theology of Liberation*, published in 1971.

We Drink from Our Own Wells is a book on spirituality that flows from that earlier work. The title is borrowed from Bernard of Clairvaux's observation that "Everyone has to drink from his own well"—that is, must be nourished by his or her own life experience.

Gutiérrez begins by questioning the basis for spiritualities in the past. In previous times, in his view, spirituality served the needs of specialized groups in the church—clerics, people in religious orders, and those "striving for perfection"—rather than the masses. If salvation and freedom are God's wish for all, then spirituality must embrace the good of all people, he says. Secondly, according to Gutiérrez, spirituality has been imagined as an individual journey to God, in which people are urged to nurture their "interior lives." In contrast to this, Gutiérrez believes we must build a social spirituality, in which growth in grace depends on our ability to reach out and contribute to a just society.

A truly contemporary and liberating spirituality, says Gutiérrez, must be a spirituality of life—and by "life" Gutiérrez has a wider context in mind than North American factions for whom being "pro-life" means only one thing. Latin Americans often face societies where murder and oppression are governmental policies. For them the fabric of life in its fullness depends on political and economic freedom.

It is their *experience* of being poor and oppressed that empowers the masses of Latin America to develop a spirituality of liberation. This is the well they drink from.

Their experience is a challenge to people in the fully industrialized countries who do not live in that situation. In Gutiérrez's words, it "invites Christians to leave the familiar world they have long inhabited, and leads many of them to reread their own spiritual tradition. Above all, it is a question of making our own the world of the poor. . . . Otherwise we shall be traveling a road that simply parallels that taken by oppressed believers."

In the middle sections of his book Gutiérrez explores the scriptural roots of liberation spirituality. He finds grounding in Paul, who placed the Spirit of Christ above the law. He also finds parallels in the Exodus story when Israel escaped from Egypt as a people, not as individuals.

The final section of the book leans on experiences of Latin American people to unpack the basic Christian themes of conversion, grace, joy, simplicity, and community.

In some respects the book is dated. Gutiérrez refers vaguely to "what is happening among us today" in Latin America. Yet because the body of the book was written more than two decades ago (the introduction was updated more recently), one is not sure which events he is referring to. So *We Drink from Our Own Wells* is less valuable as a sociopolitical analysis than for the spiritual themes it develops. And these continue to be insightful and timely.

WHY I AM STILL
A CHRISTIAN

(1985 ✦ Theology)

HANS KÜNG

(born 1928)

In 1974 Hans Küng's book *On Being a Christian* was first published, and in it the Swiss theologian argued for the absolute
necessity of religious faith, and in particular the faith that was
proclaimed and lived out by Jesus of Nazareth. The book was a
brave personal testament on Küng's part given the fact that he was
facing an investigation by his church, leading in 1979 to the loss
of his license to teach Catholic theology for questioning the doctrine of papal infallibility. Another person might have been left
embittered, but that wasn't Küng's way.

About ten years later Küng issued another personal statement,
Why I Am Still a Christian, echoing the earlier book in a more suc-
cinct and pointed manner. Without quite saying so, he addresses
this later work to the population, and particularly the youth, of an
increasingly secularized Europe, warning that by turning its back
on Christianity Europe has also been jettisoning a system of values that allowed it to function as a society. "There is no unconditionally binding moral humane action and no unconditionally
binding ethic without religion," he states, adding that without a
minimum degree of consensus about values, it is impossible for
human beings to live together, questionable whether a state can
function, or a legal system dispense justice.

The historic consensus that bound Europe together as late as
the twentieth century is now gone, he says, leaving a "profound
and far-reaching crisis of values." Young people who feel their lives

have no meaning turn to delinquency, extremist religious sects, political fanaticism, even terrorism.

Küng makes it absolutely clear that by urging a return to "religion" he is not asking people to become institutional puppets. Distinguishing between "nominally Christian and truly Christian," Küng faults his own church for the way it tries to legislate sexuality, treat divorced and remarried people, subordinate women, and exercise power generally. "If we want to be Christian," he says, "we cannot demand freedom and human rights for the church externally and not grant them internally. . . . Justice and freedom can't be preached only when it costs the church and its leaders nothing."

So why is he still a Christian? Küng mentions three reasons: First, because he feels "fundamentally positive" about the deepest traditions of Christianity. Second, because he is able to distinguish between that tradition and the present structures of the church. And third, because "I find in Christianity a basic orientation on the questions of the great Whence and Whither, Why and Wherefore of humanity and the world." Christianity, he says, is still his spiritual home.

Why I Am Still a Christian is a moving testament and persuasive in its plea for a return to religious values in society. Nevertheless, it is guilty of a certain Eurocentrism; the United States, for example, is not nearly as alienated from religion as Europe. And Küng talks about a "return" to Christian values as if the other traditions, like Judaism, Islam, Hinduism, Buddhism, did not exist.

But since this book was published Küng started the Global Ethic Foundation to encourage interreligious dialogue about human rights, freedom, justice, peace, and the world environment.

LIFE IN A JEWISH FAMILY

(1986 ✦ Autobiography)

EDITH STEIN

(1891–1942)

E dith Stein wrote this book in 1933, but it was not published until 1986. She was born into a middle-class Jewish family in Breslau, then part of Prussia, now Poland. Her father died when Edith was two, and her mother had to take over the family lumber business to provide for seven children. They weren't wealthy, but they got by. The children did well in school. They went to the synagogue, observed the holy days, and were happy.

Edith was a reserved, sometimes moody, young woman, but precocious. As a teenager she read Spinoza's *Ethics* and announced that she had become an atheist, an "independent person." She grew up to study with Edmund Husserl, then Germany's most influential philosopher. Upon graduation she could not get a teaching job at the university because she was a woman, so she became a freelance lecturer and writer.

When Stein was thirty she picked up a copy of Teresa of Avila's autobiography. Reading it totally transformed her. She was baptized a Catholic the next year. In 1933 she realized her long-sought desire to enter the Carmelite order, taking the name of Teresa Benedicta of the Cross. However, the Nazi noose was growing tighter around European Jews every year. In August 1942 Stein was deported from a convent in the Netherlands where she had sought refuge. What happened after that is hazy. It is believed she was transported almost immediately to the gas chamber.

In 1998 Edith Stein was declared by the Catholic church to be a saint and a martyr.

Stein wrote *Life in a Jewish Family* in Breslau while preparing to enter the convent. In transition from one life to another, she wanted to celebrate her Jewish and family roots. But the narrative—ostensibly about her family—is really her own story. It covers the period between her birth and 1916 when she earned a PhD *summa cum laude* from the university in Freiburg. The narrative relates family events—births and deaths, friendships, travels, studies. On its surface, it is a story of achievement. Overshadowing these sunny events, though, is the outcome of her life, which we know and the author does not.

Because this written account ends before her conversion, we don't have that part of the story to reflect on. There are hints, however. For instance, Stein, while still an agnostic, is visiting Frankfurt with a friend. They enter the Dom, and Stein recalls,

"While we looked around in respectful silence, a woman carrying a market basket came in and knelt down in one of the pews to pray briefly. This was something entirely new to me. To the synagogues or to the Protestant churches which I had visited, one went only for services. But here was someone interrupting her everyday shopping errands to come into this church, although no other person was in it, as though she were here for an intimate conversation. I could never forget that."

Some readers find the current English-language edition of Stein's *Life* physically not well designed, making it difficult for them to get into the story. But once past the details of Stein's grandparents and great-grandparents, the narrative picks up steam. By the time you reach Stein's adventures as a volunteer nurse during World War I you are fully immersed. But should you check the map in the back of the book you will suddenly notice that her hospital at Weisskirchen is just a short distance from Auschwitz where Stein would meet her death. Then the whole horrific story falls into place.

OPEN MIND, OPEN HEART

(1986 ◆ Spirituality)

THOMAS KEATING

(born 1923)

It used to be called, simply, contemplation, but in the last twenty years the name most often given to the practice of resting quietly in God's presence is "centering prayer." This method of prayer was pioneered and popularized by Cistercian monks at St. Joseph's Abbey in Spencer, Massachusetts—although, in fact, it is as old as Christendom itself.

In *Open Mind, Open Heart* Thomas Keating, the former abbot of Spencer, offers a theological, historical, and practical introduction to centering prayer. He is an excellent guide, being both aware of the spiritual tradition and sensitive to the human foibles that often cloud our relationship with God and get in the way of prayer.

After an opening chapter on what centering prayer is *not*—not a relaxation exercise, not a charismatic gift, not a parapsychological or mystical undertaking—Keating states that the root of prayer is interior silence. We don't stop thinking and feeling; we detach ourselves from thoughts and feelings. Our minds and hearts are lifted to God, but it is God who does the lifting.

Keating points out that in the early Christian centuries contemplation was considered the usual way of prayer for everyone, clergy and laity alike. By the fifteenth and sixteenth centuries, however, prayer methods had became compartmentalized. Meditation was turned into an intellectual exercise, i.e., thinking thoughts about God. Not even the genius of Ignatius Loyola, with his emphasis on affectivity, could move prayer out of the thinking mode. Henceforth, pure contemplation—prayer without images or thoughts—was prescribed only for a select few. It was certainly not considered a proper prayer for laity.

All of that changed, Keating declares, with the recovery of centering prayer. The balance of his book is devoted to practical matters: How to begin contemplation; finding a suitable place and posture; using what Keating calls a "sacred word" to focus one's prayer; and, not least important, how to deal with thoughts and distractions that inevitably arise in spite of ourselves.

These later sections of the book are obviously the fruit of workshops Keating has given over the years. (Contemplative Outreach is an organization founded by him to advance the practice of centering prayer.)

Each section leads off with a few pages of general comments, and then questions arise from an unseen audience. Fascinating questions. Can drugs enhance contemplation? Isn't it sometimes frightening to let go of all thinking and feeling? If one is aware of not thinking, isn't this awareness itself a thought? Keating's answers to these questions are invariably gentle, yet challenging.

Ultimately contemplation leads to what Keating calls "unloading the unconscious." In the light of contemplation we become aware of our many defects and the tyranny of our "false self." Sometimes we feel like we are going backward, but the process is really a path to purification. We don't push feelings away, but neither do we honor them—we just stay in God's presence.

SELECTED STORIES

(1988 ✦ Fiction)

ANDRE DUBUS

(1936–1999)

On a July evening in 1986 Andre Dubus, one of America's finest short-story writers, stopped his car somewhere in Massachusetts to help another motorist, and was struck by a third vehicle. Critically injured, he wound up losing one leg and the use of the other.

The accident changed everything in his life, including his writing. In an interview with the *National Catholic Reporter*, Dubus suggested that maybe God was trying to tell him something. "Probably," he said, "God thought I needed some editing." But then he confessed, "I don't enjoy this, but maybe I'm getting closer to God. Maybe I'll become a better person. It would be nice to get old and saintly."

Dubus never got old, dying a year after the interview. However, his work did get more layered and reflective. His *Selected Stories*, which contains work from before and after the accident, opens with several quotes, including one from Luke's gospel: "If your eyes are sound, your whole body will be filled with light." And another from his physical therapist: "You have to be lying flat on your back to look straight up."

Body images keep recurring in Dubus's stories. "The Fat Girl" tells of Louise, a young woman who, through great effort, lost seventy pounds, became svelte, married, had a baby, but emotionally missed her old, comfortable body. Eventually she gains most of the weight back and faces the breakup of her marriage but is happy with herself.

In "Miranda Over the Valley," a Boston college student finds that she is pregnant by her boyfriend back home. Miranda wants to keep the baby and marry the boy. Her parents urge her to get an abortion, and her boyfriend, with a shrug, concurs. At the end of the story, having aborted the baby, Miranda leaves him and reflects dully that "I am not for this world . . . Or it isn't for me."

It is not young women but fathers who really dominate Dubus's fiction. He had six children of his own. The typical father in his stories always goes down the sledding hill before his kids, to make sure they won't get hurt. In the summer he tests the surf for undertow. A father will go to any length for his children, and a father's faith is larger than ordinary human belief.

As one of his characters says, "Belief is believing in God; faith is believing that God believes in you."

"A Father's Story," which ends the collection, is narrated by a divorced father who has found peace living alone. Suddenly he is forced to go to the aid of an adult daughter, risking everything in the process. To God, the father admits he would not have done it for one of his sons.

> "Why? [God asks] Do you love them less?
> I tell Him no, it is not that I love them less, but that I could bear the pain of watching and knowing my sons' pain, could bear it with pride as they took the whip and nails. But You never had a daughter, and, if You had, You could not have borne her passion.
> So, [God says], you love her more than you love Me.
> I love her more than truth.
> Then you love in weakness, He says.
> As You love me, I say. . . . "

SELECTED POETRY

(1989 ✦ Poetry)

JESSICA POWERS
(1905–1988)

Jessica Powers believed in taking risks. They were not necessarily poetical risks, for her poems are conventional and straightforward. It was as a person that she took risks, and her poems celebrate the fact over and over. Consider these lines from "Counsel for Silence":

> Here you are pilgrim with no ties of earth.
> Walk out alone and make the never-told
> your healing distance and your anchorhold.
> And let the ravens feed you.

In her own life she took this risk, leaving her family and a budding career as a poet to become Sister Miriam of the Holy Spirit, a Carmelite nun in Wisconsin. In "Letter of Departure" she wrote, "There is nothing in the valley, or home, or street worth turning back for—/nothing!" Henceforth she would be a person of prayer, although prayer, too, is risky. She faced that risk as bravely as she faced the first one. As she described it in "If You Have Nothing,"

> No gift is proper to a Deity; . .
> If you have nothing, gather back your sigh,
> and with your hands held high, your heart held high,
> lift up your emptiness!

Jessica Powers was her family name and the name she used on books. She was raised on a farm in Mauston, Wisconsin, attended

Marquette University, and then, after her father died, spent eleven years back on the farm taking care of her brothers. She was writing poems even then, but she really began to grow as a writer when she spent four years in New York as a nanny and meeting other poets.

As it turned out, the farm girl hated the city. She complained in "The Uninvited," "It is a city without seed or flower, /estranged from every bird and butterfly." In "Morning of Fog" she called it "a city of phantoms," lamenting, "I am lost /in a place where nothing that beats with life should /roam."

By this time she was determined to enter Carmel, which she did in 1941, around the same time Thomas Merton was entering Gethsemane. She remained there for the rest of her life, writing poetry and serving two terms as prioress.

In the shape of her poems and in her poetical voice, Powers owes much to Emily Dickinson and Edna St. Vincent Millay. One can also hear in her verse echoes of the psalms chanted every day in her convent; in her poem "The Monastic Song" Powers relished "the strong chaste nudity of song."

In subject matter her poems reflect the everydayness of the Carmelite life: silence, nature, desire for God, and the continuing challenge of prayer. Even for Carmelites prayer can be a problem, as she remarks in "There Is a Homelessness":

. . . it is the grief of all those praying
in finite words to an Infinity
Whom, if they saw, they could not comprehend;
Whom they cannot see.

The Selected Poetry of Jessica Powers was readied for the press shortly before Sister Miriam died in 1988. Many of the poems bear dates showing when they were written, which helps in understanding them. The volume is further enhanced by a chronology of Powers's life.

MARIETTE IN ECSTASY

(1991 ✦ Fiction)

RON HANSEN

(born 1947)

A seventeen-year-old girl enters the convent as a new member of the Sisters of the Crucifixion in upstate New York. We see her kneeling at a prie-dieu. We notice her loveliness, her long brown hair, her white skin as she exchanges the elegant gown she wore on arrival for a postulant's rough habit. It is late summer in 1906. Outside, a hawk sails in the sky. In the dim chapel, the sisters file into their choir stalls to begin Terce. One of them sneaks a glance at the new postulant, Mariette. The psalms begin, *"Miserere mei Deus . . ."*

There is no place more austere, less sensuous than a contemplative cloister, and yet Ron Hansen, who teaches writing at Santa Clara University, offers it to us as an accumulation of sense experiences—its many smells, sounds, minutely observed scenes, the click of the beads, the hush of the habits, a sigh amidst the stillness. We notice small things, just as the sisters notice things about Mariette. She is a good postulant—obedient to the rule, educated, well mannered, hardworking, devout in prayer—to such an extent that she calls attention to herself, which is not good. And something else: Jesus talks to her. When she prays she sometimes falls into ecstasy.

The outer reaches of religious experience are rarely treated in fiction. Most people shrink from the idea of relishing penance or desiring pain, even for the sake of God. We are instinctively skeptical of visions and miraculous wounds. Ron Hansen doesn't tell us whether or not Mariette's experiences are genuine. It is something we, and the sisters in the convent, must find out. We perceive that the line between religious and sensuous ecstasy is very thin. Perhaps her experiences are sexual. Perhaps she is masochistic. She insists her name be pronounced not "Mare-i-ette, like a horse," but "Mariette, like a flaw."

People within the convent are divided in their opinions of the new postulant; some believe her, others do not. The convent's chaplain and confessor, Fr. Henri Marriott, initiates an investigation. Evidence is offered that Mariette is deceiving the sisters; or perhaps she is naive and fooling even herself. Against this, many sisters are sure she is a favored one of God. Exclaims one sister, "Christ shines from her. She is Christian perfection. She is lovely in every way."

It comes down to a meeting in the prioress's suite. Mariette's father, the town doctor, is there, and the prioress, and the chaplain. They examine her body for wounds. They peel bloody bandages from her palms to reveal unmarked flesh. Mariette explains, "Christ took back the wounds."

At last the prioress must decide whether Mariette will stay or go.

Mariette in Ecstasy unfolds in brief scenes from August of one year to Lent in the next, passing before us like flash cards. We are given glimpses, nothing more.

This a short novel, beautifully written, wonderfully controlled. Reading it, we are pulled between making and withholding judgment, until, in the end, we just watch events unfold and wonder at them.

A MARGINAL JEW

(1991 ◆ Theology/Scripture)

JOHN P. MEIER

(born 1942)

Could Jesus Christ read and write? Did he have any schooling? What language did he speak? Was he actually a carpenter? Did he have any brothers and sisters? Was he married?

And is any of this really important?

Most Christians—among them, most Christian scholars—would say it is. While none of these matters has direct bearing on Jesus's mission in the world, they do color popular piety about Jesus, and the way they are answered helps us understand the gospels, which are the primary documents for knowing anything at all about Jesus and his mission.

The desire to know more about the Jesus of history has engaged scholars for the past two hundred years. Prior to that it was simply assumed that the Jesus of the gospels *was* the Jesus of history. The quest was nearly abandoned when it became apparent how difficult it was to distill historical facts from the first-century faith statements that comprise the New Testament. But recent advances in archaeology, sociology, and allied sciences have given scholars new tools for reaching at least tentative historical conclusions. One of the leaders in this effort is John P. Meier, through his projected four-volume series titled *A Marginal Jew: Rethinking the Historical Jesus.*

Because of space limitations only the first volume—which considers the questions listed above—is being dealt with here. Meier makes it clear that his research will never lead us to the "real" Jesus, since that person is not accessible through historical research and never will be.

Let's follow Meier through one of the questions: Did Jesus have brothers and sisters? In years past some Catholics, in an effort to uphold Mary's perpetual virginity, argued that the persons mentioned in Mark 6:3 and Matthew 13:55 were cousins—or perhaps children of Joseph by a previous marriage (i.e., Jesus's half-brothers). Meier says the absence of siblings in the infancy narratives of Matthew and Luke make the half-brother hypothesis unlikely. And the usual meaning of *adelphos* in the Greek New Testament is blood brother, not cousin. Paul in Galatians 1:19 speaks of "James, the brother [*adelphos*] of the Lord" rather than *anepsios* (cousin). Meier points out that early Christian writers such as Hegesippus and Eusebius alluded to James as Jesus's blood brother when they could have used a more nuanced terms. "Hence," says Meier, "from a purely philological and historical point of view, the most probable opinion is that the brothers and sisters of Jesus were his siblings."

Meier's treatment of this topic is of course far more detailed than what is summarized here. Despite the complexities of argument, however, his writing is always engaging, and the questions he raises are endlessly fascinating.

Meier, a member of the theology faculty at Notre Dame, says these kinds of questions can never undermine the church's faith in Jesus, which exists on another plane altogether. Yet, he says, "no person of any religious persuasion can be considered truly educated today if he or she has not investigated to some degree what historical research can tell us about this enigmatic figure who unleashed one of the major religious and cultural forces in the world."

SHE WHO IS

(1992 ✦ Theology)

ELIZABETH A. JOHNSON

(born 1941)

Understanding who God is and how God acts in the world is a never-ending task for believers. A work in progress. Just when we think we have a handle on it, someone asks a question no one thought to ask before. The problem is not that humans are endlessly and damnably curious but that God is so *big*. We will never find enough paper to wrap this gift.

Today's believers find that classical formulations describing the Deity don't work as well as they used to. Indeed, Cardinal Walter Kasper has spoken of the "heresy of theism," as if confining oneself to traditional images of God had become dangerous to people's faith. Many questions being asked in our day arise from Christianity's encounter with other world religions, and from the challenge of Marxism, coupled with the wars and suffering of the twentieth century. Who any longer can believe in a God far above us who is isolated and distant from human affairs? Such a God no longer satisfies.

So the religious imagination has been trying to locate God within suffering humanity—no longer the Lord Ruler of history but a compassionate, relational God who weeps with the suffering and who supports those seeking freedom. At the forefront of this movement are the people who were overlooked by traditional theologies—"Third World" peoples and marginalized Christians, including women. One of the prominent women's voices belongs to Elizabeth A. Johnson, especially in her book *She Who Is: The Mystery of God in Feminist Theological Discourse.*

Johnson, a Sister of St. Joseph and Distinguished Professor of Theology at New York's Fordham University, begins by asserting that the mystery of God is ultimately beyond comprehension and surely beyond human words. That is why, she says, she wants to challenge the assumption of classical theism that God is male, "or at least more like a man than a woman, or at least more fittingly addressed as male than as female."

Just as an icon produced in India might picture the Holy Family as Asian, so all humans image God in light of their own experience. A God who perforce is male, says Johnson, can never fully represent the experience of women who constitute half of the human race. On the other hand, imaging God as "She Who Is" both validates women's experience and gives us new appreciation of the God who is compassionate, relational, and nurturing.

Johnson explores veiled references in Holy Scripture to feminine qualities in the Deity. She looks at the many names applied to God by Christians and people of other faiths. The most creative part of the book is a discussion of Sophia (or Wisdom) in the Judeo-Christian tradition as it relates to the Holy Spirit, to Jesus, and to the Creator (whom Johnson calls "Mother-Sophia").

She Who Is does not advocate jettisoning the male God in favor of a female Deity, but it does argue that there is added richness to be gained in a balanced view. The argument is detailed and the writing sometimes dense yet within the reach of the motivated reader.

This is a work of feminist theology; and while it certainly does have a prophetic edge, the book's strength comes from the fact that it is steeped in traditional Catholic belief. Elizabeth Johnson writes within the familiar landscape of Catholic theology, but she takes us down a path we may never have noticed before.

VIRGIN TIME

(1992 ✦ Spirituality)

PATRICIA HAMPL

(born 1946)

When was the last time you read a spiritual book populated by real characters? Of course the people in Thérèse of Lisieux's autobiography—her parents and sisters—are real enough, but they don't spring vividly to life the way people do in Patricia Hampl's *Virgin Time*. That's because Hampl is, first of all, a story-teller. A professor of English at the University of Minnesota, she is the author of short stories, memoirs, two volumes of poetry, and a collection of essays titled *I Could Tell You Stories*.

Virgin Time is a narrative of a pilgrimage, really a series of pil-grimages, touched off by her friendship with "Donnie" (Sister Mary Madonna), a contemplative Franciscan back in St. Paul. For a time Hampl, although the product of a Catholic household and parochial school education, had fallen away from religious practice (". . . maybe we had too much meaning too early . . ."). But when that Presence she knew as a teenager was encountered again in the sisters' quiet chapel, Hampl decided to look for it in other places—in Assisi, Lourdes, or wherever it dwelled. "I'd come to the conviction that I had to see the old world of Catholicism. More than see—to touch it."

So she joins a small band of tourists hiking over the hills of Umbria on their way to Assisi. This is where we meet the characters. Her fellow hikers, mostly British, weren't on a religious journey as Hampl was and regarded her surreptitious visits to wayside chapels with amusement and curiosity. She has her companion tourists down perfectly—their mealtime banter, their prying questions, their charming "pagan" ways. If you ever want to read an amusing spiritual book, here's your chance.

Once in Assisi Hampl meets a group of American Franciscans —priests and sisters—who are equally charming. In irreverent ways they peel away the tourist glitz to show her the true spirituality of the place and of the Franciscan calling.

But all this time what Hampl wants most is the recovery of prayer. Her book is subtitled "In Search of the Contemplative Life." She doesn't find it in Assisi or Lourdes. Only in the final section of the book, when she visits a Cistercian monastery set among the California redwoods, does her search bear fruit. There, standing in a meadow at dawn, watching light spread across the sky, Hampl experiences what Thomas Merton called "the virgin point between darkness and light, between being and nonbeing."

She writes, "I understood prayer is, after all, a plain statement of fact. An admission of existence. That's all. A surrender of self to the All of history and oblivion. Surrender of intention into the truth of a life. You don't get to live Life—that thing I feared I was missing. You just live a life. This one."

Virgin Time is alternately funny, informative, provocative, and moving. It takes the form of a travel book, in the way that all pilgrimage accounts are essentially travel books—in which the outer journey is a metaphor for an inner one. Like most pilgrims, Patricia Hampl doesn't always know where she is going, but she knows what she is looking for, and knows when she has found it.

DEAD MAN WALKING

(1993 ✦ Memoir)

HELEN PREJEAN
(born 1939)

Many of us have seen the movie, but we should also read the book. Sister Helen Prejean's account of ministering to death-row murderers is as powerful on paper as it was on film. When it appeared in 1993 the book version was widely praised, spent thirty-one weeks on the *New York Times* bestseller list, and was nominated for the Pulitzer Prize. In the years since, Prejean has received numerous honorary degrees from universities in the United States and Europe, and many awards honoring not only her courage as a minister but her efforts to end the death penalty in the United States.

The book *Dead Man Walking* is significantly different from the film. The movie focused exclusively on the author's relationship with Patrick Sonnier leading up to his death in the Louisiana electric chair in 1984. That story occupies only the first half of the book. Later chapters describe her ministry to Robert Lee Willie, executed that same year, and to Vernon and Elizabeth Harvey, parents of the young woman Willie brutally killed.

Prejean's relationship with the Harveys is a fascinating story in itself. After the Sonnier execution, Prejean was determined not to forget the victims of violent crimes. She contacted Mr. and Mrs. Harvey soon after she became spiritual advisor to their daughter's killer. At first the relationship was polite but wary. Vernon Harvey was adamantly in favor of the death penalty and expressed his ardent desire to watch Robert Lee Willie "fry" for his crimes. While they never changed each other's minds, Prejean and the

Harveys eventually grew in respect and became warm friends. In time their connection led Prejean to start a ministry for the victims of violent crime.

In addition to these accounts, *Dead Man Walking* surveys the history and legal background of the death penalty as it is presently applied in America. The book weighs the biblical evidence for and against capital punishment and reviews doctrinal statements by the Vatican and by the United States bishops. It comments on the "eye-for-an-eye" justification often cited by people in favor of executions, noting that the Bible means those words to limit, not permit, retribution.

In telling the stories of Patrick Sonnier and Robert Lee Willie, Prejean also describes the effect executions have on prison personnel—on the guards, wardens, and public officials whose job it is to put people to death. Almost invariably they are psychologically scarred by the experience. While they may begin by supporting it, those forced to see executions close-up often develop reservations about the whole process.

Prejean makes the point over and over again that capital punishment in the United States is closely linked to race and poverty. It's the poor who are put to death, especially the African American poor. Middle-class and Caucasian criminals are far more likely to be sentenced to prison. And the average time served for the typical "life" sentence in the United States is slightly more than six years. So only the poor die; the rest have the opportunity to be reintegrated into society.

Reading *Dead Man Walking* is an eye-opening experience. When you are done with it you will never feel the same about the death penalty, and, in addition, you will through her words have met a remarkable woman.

CROSSING THE
THRESHOLD OF HOPE

(1994 ✦ *Theology*)

POPE JOHN PAUL II
(1920–2005)

In 1993 Italian journalist Vittorio Messori arranged to interview Pope John Paul II on television as a way of marking the fifteenth anniversary of the pope's election. As it turned out, scheduling conflicts doomed the television program, but the pope was intrigued by the questions Messori submitted in advance, so he sat down and wrote responses. This was the genesis of the book published as *Crossing the Threshold of Hope*. For the pope, who was a published author many times over, this one proved to be an international bestseller.

It's easy to understand why the pope was caught up by the questions, because they raise serious religious issues and apply them to the pope's own life: How does the pope pray? Doesn't it verge on scandal to elevate one Christian above all the rest? Why is there so much evil in the world? Is Jesus the Son of God? How does Christianity relate to Judaism, to Islam, to Buddhism? Was God at work in the collapse of Communism? And what is the whole point in religious belief anyway?

In all, thirty-five topics are covered, some of them questions within questions. The pope's responses generally begin with a broad view of the issue, trying to give it historical and theological perspective. Sometimes they are little homilies. But the pope always comes around to the core question, and his answers are sometimes surprising.

Why is God silent? Why doesn't God come closer to people? The pope responds: God has come as close as possible. People can't tolerate too much closeness.

Does the Roman Catholic church alone offer salvation to people? John Paul: It is Jesus who offers salvation. The church is just a vehicle in this process. The mystery of God's church is far, far bigger than the Roman church.

Did God cause Communism to fail? The pope: No, it collapsed from its own incompetence.

Crossing the Threshold of Hope is labeled here as a work of theology. While not theology in an academic sense, the book gives John Paul II an opportunity to teach, explain, and comment at length on the church tradition. He is an erudite man, fully acquainted with twentieth-century philosophy. He makes passing reference to Ludwig Wittgenstein (distinguishing between his early and his late works), Paul Ricoeur, Martin Buber, André Malraux, Albert Camus, to list just a few. One definitely has the sense the pope didn't employ aides to fill in these sources—he knew his material.

Naturally the pope can also quote scripture and the church fathers to good effect. The number of times he refers to the Second Vatican Council is astonishing. This was a pope who, according to unfriendly critics, tried to deconstruct the council's effect. But council documents abound in this book, and they are always presented in a positive light. John Paul reflects happily on his participation at the council and the support given him there by key figures like Yves Congar and Henri de Lubac.

Crossing the Threshold of Hope is in every way a remarkable book— a book to learn from and a pleasure to read.

HOW THE IRISH
SAVED CIVILIZATION

(1995 ✦ History)

THOMAS CAHILL

(born 1940)

Visiting Ireland in the nineteenth century, British historian Charles Kingsley deplored "the human chimpanzees I saw" in that "horrible country." Had they been black-skinned, he said, it would not have been so bad, "but their skins, except where tanned by exposure, are as white as ours."

Kingsley's contempt and loathing for the Irish people was not unusual among the upper classes in that era; some of it lingers still. It is with a certain relish, then, that Thomas Cahill gives us a book describing how Catholic Ireland became a repository of learning during the so-called barbarian invasions. He clearly takes delight in titling his account *How the Irish Saved Civilization*.

Cahill, a scholar of art and literature and onetime director of religious publishing at Doubleday, opens his story by recounting the decrepitude and eventual breakup of the Roman Empire—which he says was not the fault of Christianity, as Edward Gibbon maintained in his *Decline and Fall*, but simply the result of Roman incompetence and corruption. Then he moves his gaze to Ireland, a raw Celtic settlement on the western fringe of Europe. Ireland in the early fifth century CE was far from being an effete culture like Rome. It was passionate and wild, and its people were earthy, warlike pagans. Yet within two generations after Patricus (Patrick) arrived to preach the Christian gospel in 432, the island was converted. It gave up its ferocious ways, or most of them. Monasticism flourished. And when the nomadic invaders careened through Europe, looting and burning its cultural treasures, it was the Irish, far off in the west, who kept the flame of learning alive. They were joined by European monks fleeing the continent, bringing their sacred books with them. Irish monasteries copied them furiously. Indeed, says Cahill of that period, "Ireland stood in the position of becoming Europe's publisher."

And when, after a century or so, devastated Europe achieved a measure of peace, monks from Ireland went back to the continent to re-Christianize the population, establish schools and monasteries, and supply them with books. Alcuin, a Northumbrian monk trained by the Irish, became an advisor to the Emperor Charlemagne and founder of a school that over the centuries evolved into the University of Paris. Boniface became the apostle to Germany, and the eccentric Columbanus founded monasteries in Gaul and as far south as Lombardy.

The Irish were learned not only in the sacred sciences—some of them could read Greek, and an Irish layman, John Scotus Eriugena, was "the first philosopher of the Middle Ages," according to Cahill. And he had a wicked tongue. He was sitting across the table from Emperor Charles the Bald one evening when the emperor challenged him with a riddle: "What separates a fool from an Irishman?" Replied Eriugena, "Only the table."

How the Irish Saved Civilization is rich with anecdotes. The book is memorable, too, for the sensitive way it describes the blending of Christianity and the Celtic religions. The Celts believed the gods spoke to them through nature, but their gods were bloodthirsty and dark. The native people welcomed Patrick's assurance that Christ had relieved them of the blood debt.

Writes Thomas Cahill, "This magical world, though full of adventure and surprise, is no longer full of dread. Rather, Christ has trodden all pathways before us, and at every crossroads and by every tree the Word of God speaks out. We have only to be quiet and listen. . . ."

AN AMERICAN REQUIEM

(1996 ◆ Memoir)

JAMES CARROLL

(born 1943)

Catholics like to think they are a people united in faith—as indeed they are, except for those times when they are divided by faith. Divisions among them arise from the many styles of being Catholic and by paradoxes that abide at the heart of the Christian message. In Matthew's gospel Jesus says, "blessed are the peacemakers" but later announces, "I have not come to bring peace, but a sword." Faith statements that seem to contradict each other are used as ammunition in culture wars, such as those that raged through the Catholic church in the last few decades. No book better captures the passion and pain of those struggles than James Carroll's elegiac memoir *An American Requiem: God, My Father, and the War that Came Between Us.*

James Carroll today is an acclaimed novelist living in Boston with his wife and two children. In 1969 he was ordained a Catholic priest, served for a time as a chaplain at Boston University, and was active in resistance to the Vietnam War. Later he left the priesthood. That part of his story was acted out many times in the post–Vatican II church.

Yet Carroll's story had another layer: His father, Joseph Carroll, was an Air Force general who selected targets for American bombs in Vietnam. The senior Carroll was himself a devout Catholic who had studied for the priesthood but left before ordination and who surely looked to his son to reclaim some part of a lost vocation. General Carroll was a trusted confidant of FBI Director J. Edgar Hoover; James Carroll, on the other hand, participated in a mock trial that convicted Hoover of war crimes. Both the father and the son were passionate believers who felt compelled to pursue their faith in ways that strained and gnawed at the family bond between them.

Much of *An American Requiem* is a coming-of-age story that recounts a happy family, upwardly mobile, and the often-inarticulate love of Joseph Carroll for his children. The senior Carroll enjoyed a meteoric career, rising from a Chicago stockyards worker to a lawyer to an FBI agent who was elevated to a high position in the Bureau and later in the Pentagon. One day the family was living in a modest apartment in Arlington, Virginia; the next day their home was a mansion in Wiesbaden, Germany, with chauffeurs and servants at their elbows and senators and cardinals as their guests. The Carroll family had a private audience with Pope John XXIII, who gave young James his personal blessing.

But if the Carrolls were a poster family for the coming-of-age of American Catholicism, they also harbored the seeds of its discord and its clouded agenda in the era of the Cold War. As James Carroll laments, he and his father had the opportunity and the weapons to break each other's hearts. Their story, which won the National Book Award for nonfiction in 1996, is a reminder that even culture wars can have collateral casualties.

AN INTRODUCTION TO
THE NEW TESTAMENT

(1997 ◆ Theology/Scripture)

RAYMOND E. BROWN

(1928–1998)

The last hundred years have witnessed a virtual revolution in the way Christians have approached their Holy Scriptures. New advances in the fields of linguistics, history, and archaeology have made it possible to read the Bible with eyes that are educated as well as pious. It is not unusual today to hear scholars and even ordinary Christians ask, What did the original author mean in a particular passage? What was going on at the time it was written? To what extent are Bible stories rooted in ancient myths and fables?

The Catholic church was originally suspicious of such questions. In the nineteenth century it lumped critical approaches to the Bible in with other movements of "Modernism" and roundly condemned them. The real advances in scripture scholarship were left to Protestants. Then in the twentieth century all that was changed. Pope Pius XII in his encyclical *Divino Afflante Spiritu* (1943) opened the door to historical-critical scholarship, making it possible for the church gradually to back away from biblical fundamentalism. When after Vatican II the church put more scripture into Sunday worship, grassroots Bible study blossomed, making Catholics among the world's most scripturally literate.

An Introduction to the New Testament by Raymond E. Brown is representative of the high standards of Catholic biblical scholarship at the turn of the millennium. During his lifetime Brown was ranked among the world's foremost New Testament scholars. He was a member of the Pontifical Biblical Commission, and taught for many years at Union Theological Seminary, founded by Protestants. He was a scholar of the first rank yet was sensitive to the needs of beginning students and ordinary laity. His book manages to serve all those ends.

This introduction, however, is not light reading. Brown's book is a magisterial survey, over eight hundred pages in length, and covers general topics such as inspiration, hermeneutics (the study and art of interpretation), the political and social backgrounds of the first century CE, religious and political history, and then each New Testament book in detail.

The treatment of a typical book considers its literary style, its intended audience, date of composition, a general analysis of its message, and its theology, among other topics. On the subject of authorship, Brown—along with many scholars—questions whether the Apostle Paul wrote the letters to the Colossians and Ephesians and does not believe the Apostle John wrote the fourth gospel or the book of Revelation. Who did? Read Brown and find out.

In the course of his career, Brown staked out a position for himself as a "centrist" scholar—neither progressive nor conservative—and this book reflects that stance. He believed that not everything in the New Testament is literally true (the Bethlehem story, for instance, is just a story), but he maintained that the New Testament contains no error in matters pertaining to salvation.

Brown's *Introduction* belongs on the shelf of every library and of every serious student of the New Testament.

ALL SAINTS

(1997 ✦ Biography)

ROBERT ELLSBERG
(born 1955)

After the Bible, the most popular Christian stories have been the lives of the saints. In the first centuries the persecuted Christian minority circulated word-of-mouth stories about Sebastian, Agnes, Ignatius of Antioch, and the holy martyrs. Likewise in the Middle Ages pilgrims entertained each other on the road with tales about Martin of Tours, George the Dragonslayer, and Elizabeth of Hungary. In modern times the stories have tended to focus on missionaries, mystics, and social activists.

Very early in church history saint stories became a literary genre. At first there was the *Martyrology*, a collection of gory and often improbable accounts of the slaughter of early Christians. The trend continued with medieval miracle plays and poems. A high tide of sorts was achieved in the eighteenth century with the publication of *Lives of the Fathers, Martyrs and Other Principal Saints* by Alban Butler (1710–1773), an English priest living in France. Butler mined classical sources for 1,600 stories published in four volumes. His work was a considerable achievement, but to modern eyes his accounts lean toward hagiography.

Recent years have seen changes in the Catholic perception of saints. First, the number of official saints has grown significantly, especially during the pontificate of Pope John Paul II, when more holy people from Eastern Europe and developing countries were canonized. Second, Catholics have come to acknowledge true saints outside the ranks of the canonized. People like Dorothy

Day, Martin Luther King, Jr., as well as non-Christians such as Mohandas Gandhi have been raised up as models of the holy life.

A book that captures this new spirit is Robert Ellsberg's *All Saints*. Ellsberg, the editor in chief of Orbis Books, says he included in the book "men and women whose lives and message . . . speak to the spiritual needs of the day." He adds, "By exploring a range of lives far beyond the official canon of saints, I hope to expand the popular understanding of holiness itself."

Included in his list of sacred lives are people such as Galileo, artist Georges Rouault, theologian Henri de Lubac, Oskar Schindler, novelist Flannery O'Connor, and even Alban Butler—the hagiographer now hagiographed. The book's subjects, 365 of them, are assigned to days of the year, creating the effect of a traditional calendar of saints.

Ellsberg's mixture of contemporary and historical figures with canonical saints is both powerful and moving. His approach is reverent without being adoring. The principle of selection that seems to have shaped the book is faithfulness to the beatitudes. These are men and women who in their lifetimes worked for justice, strove for peace, and lived selfless lives of compassion. One can read *All Saints* to learn more about these holy people or to inspire one's own heart to serve others. Like the saint stories of old, these sacred lives continue to work their magic on us.

SAINTS AND SINNERS

(1997 ◆ History)

EAMON DUFFY

(born 1947)

There can't be Catholicism as we know it without popes. Telling their long history would normally require many volumes, but Eamon Duffy, the distinguished Professor of the History of Christianity at Magdalene College, Cambridge, has done it with éclat and firm judgment in just one.

Subtitled "A History of the Popes," the book is an offshoot of a six-part television series in Britain. It tracks the popes and their ups and downs through six historical eras: the establishment of the papacy in the first five hundred years; the so-called Dark Ages and the Carolingian empire; the medieval period; the Renaissance and Reformation; the Enlightenment and early modern era; and, finally, the twentieth century when the popes became, in Duffy's phrase, "the oracles of God."

Popular belief holds that there has been a continual line of popes from Peter to John Paul II, but Duffy is quick to point out there is little evidence of that in the first three centuries. Roman Christians claimed succession—as a church—from Peter, but it is not clear that succession rested in one particular person. Even after the line of bishops in Rome was firmly established, they were not recognized as popes with jurisdiction over the universal church. It was only with Leo the Great (440–461) that the papacy was firmly identified with the authority of Peter.

Those early popes were referees more than monarchs, settling disputes among lesser bishops and seeking firm ground in the constantly shifting world of schisms and heresies. They hewed to an orthodox Christian line against the Arians and Monophysites—a delicate task when the rulers of the Eastern empire tended to favor the suspect doctrines. In the end the popes won out, but Duffy makes it sound like a very close call.

As suggested by the title, *Saints and Sinners* doesn't spare the Renaissance popes: Alexander VI, for instance, who kept a mistress in the Vatican, and Leo X who was made a cardinal at the age of thirteen and who sold indulgences so recklessly he set off the Protestant Reformation. The Renaissance popes invariably advanced their own families but also did much to rebuild Rome, which had fallen into decrepitude—and, of course, they patronized the arts. Yet, Duffy says, by the seventeenth century "all good men recognized that something would have to be done about the popes."

The Council of Trent brought reform but also made the papacy an avid player in the age of absolutism. Popes like Urban VIII became as rigid as the most absolute monarch.

Some readers will be most interested in Duffy's take on the modern popes: Pius IX who pursued what Cardinal Manning called "the beauty of inflexibility," Pius X who vowed to "unmask the rot of liberalism" in the church, the anti-Nazism of Pius XI, and Pius XII's delicate dance with totalitarianism. John XXIII draws praise for being unconventional, and Paul VI and Vatican II for "redrawing the boundaries of what had seemed to be a fixed and immutable system." Duffy pulls his punches on John Paul II, still in office when this book was written, but remarks on the pontiff's "boundless energy."

Anyone who wants to know how the church got to be where it is today will want to read Eamon Duffy's history of the popes.

THE MINISTRY OF RECONCILIATION

(1998 ◆ *Spirituality*)

ROBERT J. SCHREITER

(born 1947)

What the world needs now is reconciliation. People everywhere thirst for it. Civil discourse is nearly eradicated by conflicts between jihadists and the Western democracies, haves and have-nots, pro-lifers and pro-choicers, liberals and conservatives, not to mention you and me. Acknowledging it and doing something about, however, are two different things. How are we supposed to forget old wrongs, and who takes the first step?

Reconciliation that involves large populations rather than individuals is especially difficult. In recent years, however, progress has been made by truth and reconciliation movements in South Africa and Latin America. In *The Ministry of Reconciliation*, theologian Robert Schreiter reflects on those developments and the meaning of reconciliation from a Christian perspective.

In a wonderful first chapter, Schreiter outlines a spirituality of reconciliation that is both scriptural and informed by what has happened in places like South Africa. He begins with the assertion that reconciliation is always God's work, not ours. We assume that wrongdoers will repent, but that is rarely the first step. "God begins with the victim," he says, "restoring the victim to humanity which the wrongdoer has tried to wrest away. . . ." The victim then calls the wrongdoer to repentance and forgiveness.

The moment of reconciliation often comes upon the victim as a surprise; he never expected to go there. In the end, the experience of reconciliation makes both the victim and the wrongdoer "a new creation." They do not go back to old habits; they find themselves in a new and justified relationship.

Schreiter scorns the old maxim "forgive and forget." We should forgive, he says, but we should never forget. Forgetting would whitewash history and ignore the sacrifice of those who died in the struggle. Their memory needs to be nurtured, not put aside.

The rest of the book flows from these initial insights. Schreiter, a member of the faculty of the Catholic Theological Union in Chicago, builds the subsequent chapters on the gospel readings of the Easter season. Each one, in its own way, tells how evil is overcome, what suffering and death mean, and what we may hope for from God.

For instance, the gospel story of the women and the empty tomb describes the "circle of love" they build around death. Schreiter remarks on the surprise of Mary Magdalene when she encounters Jesus in the garden. He says, "recognition is the turning point in the surprise, when the grace of reconciliation rushes into our hearts."

For Schreiter, the Road to Emmaus story is about inviting a stranger to break bread with us. Not until we try it do we discover the stranger is really Jesus.

To say that reconciliation is the work of God is not the same as saying we have no part in it. The actual moment of coming together is grace, but we need strategies to get to that moment. There is a progression within reconciliation, and the wise person will let it unfold in its natural course.

Wisdom and Robert Schreiter's book are two invaluable tools for achieving the desired end.

CHARMING BILLY

(1998 ◆ Fiction)

ALICE MCDERMOTT

(born 1953)

There is a moment in *Charming Billy* when Billy Lynch, a soldier serving in Europe during World War II, encounters a French girl who begs him to carry a message to her fiancé, another GI who had moved on. She wants him to know, "I am still here."

That moment, recalled later on a boozy night after the war, could have been a motif for Billy's own life—a life of faithful but hopeless waiting, of abandonment and missed opportunity.

After the war Billy met an Irish girl visiting Long Island and fell hopelessly in love. She had to return to Ireland, but Billy was fixated on bringing her back to the U.S. and marrying her. He sent her money for the passage. She never came. Then one day Billy learns from his cousin Dennis that the girl, Eva, has died of pneumonia. With that news, Billy—always the charmer, charismatic, handsome, a man who makes people smile when he walks into a room—is left without the one person he believes was destined for him. How does one remain "still here" when the real chance of happiness has slipped away? Billy does it by drinking. His friends and the wife he accepted in a loveless marriage take care of him, pour him into bed at night, and watch him deteriorate over the years.

What Billy doesn't know is that Dennis lied. Eva never died but married someone else in Ireland. Dennis invented the story of death by pneumonia to soften the blow on his cousin and friend.

Charming Billy is a love story of a different kind. The lovers have seemingly missed connections, but Billy can't let go of Eva's memory or their few moments in heaven together. His casual charm masks a fierce determination to be true to her. His friends and family know pieces of it and speculate about the rest. They are charmed by him even as they are nursing their own regrets and lost opportunities.

Alice McDermott's novel, which won the National Book Award for fiction in 1998, weaves together the stories of Billy and his friends—stories that punctuate, layer, and illuminate each other. McDermott knows these Irish neighborhoods of New York City where her story unfolds and where she grew up. She currently lives in Maryland, writing and teaching at Johns Hopkins University.

In an interview with Elizabeth Farnsworth on PBS, she remarked that *Charming Billy* is ultimately "a novel about faith, and what we believe in, and above all, what we choose to believe in." She went on to say,

> "I think that Billy in this community is someone who the people around him have to believe a romantic tale about. They love him so dearly and are so fond of him and . . . they've watched him destroy himself. It's not enough for them to say, 'Well, Billy's had an unfortunate life.' They need to make something more of his life. And they do that by telling stories about him. They keep the faith that his life was valuable, even though on the surface it seems only pathetic."

THE HOLY LONGING

(1998 ✦ Spirituality)

RONALD ROLHEISER

(born 1948)

Everyone who is really alive has a fire in the belly. People may not recognize it as spiritual fire. They are more likely to believe it is sexual energy, or worldly ambition, or passion for justice, or some private obsession—but its real origin is spiritual, says Ronald Rolheiser.

The Canadian priest describes how many people today have encountered "an unquenchable fire, a restlessness, a longing, a disquiet, a hunger, a loneliness, a gnawing nostalgia, a wildness that cannot be tamed, a congenital all-embracing ache that lies at the center of human existence."

Figuring out what to do with that fire is the work of spirituality.

In ages past people realized their inner longing was ultimately a desire for God, but our era is so secular we no longer make those connections, according to Rolheiser. We have lost the ability to live with our own energy. We keep sliding off in one direction or another, into wild enthusiasm or depression. Mostly depression.

Ours is the age of personal freedom, and we naively believe we can harness the inner fire all by ourselves. But the fire within is far more powerful than we imagine. We need help, he says.

The Holy Longing offers itself as a guidebook for people who have not been exposed to Christian spirituality in a way that makes it palatable. After surveying the present situation, Rolheiser lists the "nonnegotiable essentials" of good spirituality. They are private prayer, social morality, compassion (which he calls "mellowness of heart"), and a supporting community. Lack any one of those parts and one's spiritual life will be out of kilter.

The real heart of his book is Rolheiser's treatment of the incarnation as the basis for Christian spirituality. The incarnation, he says, is not a historic event in the life of Christ as much as a present reality in ours. We *are* the Body of Christ. The reality of incarnation affects the way we pray, the way we practice morality, live lives of compassion, and abide in community. The incarnation is the boundary between a theist, who believes in a heavenly God, and a Christian, who finds God in the here and now.

As a spiritual writer Ronald Rolheiser is heir to Henri Nouwen, Thomas Merton, and others who wrote for a previous generation. He is acutely sensitive to the present condition of believers and seekers and brings theological nuance to his writing. He is a member of the Oblates of Mary Immaculate and has taught at Newman Theological College in Edmonton, at Seattle University, and most recently at the Oblate School of Theology in San Antonio.

Our task as Christians, Rolheiser believes, is to "live in the interim"—between the resurrection and the final consummation of Christ. This requires a nice sense of balance and acceptance of the fact that we are not in control of events or of ourselves.

He writes, "During that time, and it is an interim time, we will always live in tension, waiting for the final consummation of history and our lives. Our happiness depends on not overcoming this [tension], which we cannot do in any case, but in making our peace with it."

THE LIBERATION
OF THE LAITY

(2002 ✦ *Theology)*

PAUL LAKELAND

(born 1946)

The early Christian church that we find in the Acts of the Apostles was supported, like a tent, by two poles: One pole was the devoted fellowship of the faithful made visible by service and mutual sharing. The other was the apostolic witness of the Twelve—the men who had seen Jesus, talked with him, and who were empowered to carry his message to the world, founding new communities as they went. However, the twin poles of fellowship and authority broke down, partly because the Roman Empire itself was breaking down. In time the fellowship pole was weakened and the authority pole strengthened, until at last the hierarchy bore all the weight of the tent and the laity none.

This was the situation that existed when Vatican Council II declared the Christian church to be "the people of God" and used words such as "collegiality" to describe the inner working of its parts. Such a view implicitly endorsed the notion of fellowship and harkened back to the two-pole era. In the wake of the council some people predicted a new "age of the laity." Others resisted it. There is no book that more effectively summarizes these changing views of the laity before and after the council and their possible projected course than Paul Lakeland's *The Liberation of the Laity.*

Lakeland, a lay member of the theology faculty at Fairfield University in Connecticut, devotes the first two chapters of his book to a theology of the laity in the years just before Vatican II. There was a great deal of groundwork being done in Europe by the Frenchmen Jean Daniélou, Henri de Lubac, and Yves Congar. Congar, especially, maintained that the "priesthood of the laity" was of a different order than the ordained priesthood, and not dependent on it. According to Lakeland, Congar believed the apostolic nature of the church resided as much in the faith of the people as in the succession of the bishops. He made the point that the whole church is apostolic, not just one part of the church.

Congar was instrumental in formulating key sections of several council documents. These advanced the ideas that all members of the church are essentially equal, share one call to holiness, and that the laity has a role in building up the church from below.

After surveying the council in more detail than can be mentioned here, Lakeland takes us through the theology of the laity in the years since the council, particularly in the writings of Edward Schillebeeckx, Leonardo Boff, and Hans Küng.

In the second half of *The Liberation of the Laity*, Lakeland becomes more prophetic and tries to outline a path into the future. Here his language becomes harsher as he uses words such as "oppression" and "a celibate caste" in talking about the clergy. Yet Lakeland has some fascinating observations on secularity, which he claims is part of a divine plan for the church. In his view the laity—the people of God—are leaven hidden in the secular world.

Ultimately, says Lakeland, "we—all of us who are baptized adults—exercise a ministry in the world by working toward the 'vision of the real' that the Catholic tradition proclaims. No one in the church calls us to that ministry. Christ calls us to it in our adult membership in his church."

THE LIFE YOU SAVE
MAY BE YOUR OWN

(2003 ◆ Biography)

PAUL ELIE
(born 1965)

It is most fitting to conclude this volume of Catholic books with one that tells the story of four great American Catholic writers. Paul Elie's *The Life You Save May Be Your Own* describes the careers and concerns of Thomas Merton, Dorothy Day, Walker Percy, and Flannery O'Connor, whose lives overlapped each other, who all knew each other's writing and in most cases also knew each other, and who did much to shape twentieth-century American Catholicism. So influential were they that they formed the core of what Carolyn Gordon dubbed "the school of the Holy Ghost."

Elie, an editor at Farrar, Straus and Giroux, intermingles their biographies, emphasizing how each in his or her own way came to grips with the meaning of faith in mid-century America. Merton, the young man who gave up secular life for "God Alone," came gradually to embrace the holiness of the ordinary. Day, the radical social reformer, spent her life witnessing to the presence of Christ in the poor, and resisting people who wanted to make her into a plaster saint. Percy, a New Orleans convert, turned his back on medicine to write philosophical novels about alienated people seeking to reconnect with life. O'Connor, the only cradle Catholic of the four, produced stories of rural people in a God-haunted world.

Encountering their stories side by side, one is struck by the differences among them as writers and the unique ways each expressed her or his own faith. Here are four people nurtured in a church that was thought to be monolithic—whose members were believed to walk in lockstep—and yet Day, O'Connor, Merton, and Percy couldn't have been more different in their approaches. They did read each other's works and in some cases exchanged letters. Merton and Day carried on a lengthy correspondence. However, Day, who loved fiction, never understood Percy's novels; she called their differences "generational."

They wrote during a time after the Second World War when religious belief was being recast. Vatican II was in process. A vast evangelical awakening was beginning to stir America. The atomic bomb and other machines of death had disenchanted many with the god of science, but few in those days saw the Christian God as a viable alternative. When at a dinner party Mary McCarthy claimed the eucharist was just a nice symbol, O'Connor shot back, "Well, if it's a symbol, to hell with it."

We read these people not in their time but ours, looking for something to keep us going in our own journey to God. Just as Dorothy Day mined the novels of Dostoyevsky for inspiration, so we look to Day, to Thomas Merton, to Flannery O'Connor and Walker Percy to be lights for our pilgrimage. As Paul Elie observes, "Certain books, certain writers, reach us at the center of ourselves, and we come to them in fear and trembling, in hope and expectation—reading so as to change, and perhaps save, our lives."

AFTERWORD:
AND FIFTY MORE

In the process of compiling a list of one hundred great books, one is always making compromises, accepting some titles and leaving out others. This afterword is a chance to acknowledge the books that didn't make the final cut, and to mention some categories of books that were not included in this volume. It would have been nice, for instance, to list some children's titles. However it is not a genre this author knows much about, so it was relatively easy to exclude them, especially when so many other books were clamoring for attention.

Nor are there any prayer books listed in the table of contents. If you are looking for collections of prayers, it is always good to start with *The Liturgy of the Hours*, published in various formats by the Catholic Book Publishing Co. One little book many have found useful is *Hearts on Fire*, edited by Michael Harter (Institute of Jesuit Sources, 1993). Edward Hays wrote a contemporary classic with his *Prayers for the Domestic Church* that celebrate family events such as arriving home from a journey, for a new child, for farm animals, etc. (Forest of Peace/Ave Maria Press, 1979). And, although it was intended for public worship, the *Book of Blessings* authorized by the American bishops is fine for families and groups (Liturgical Press, 1989, and Catholic Book Publishing Co., 1989).

There have been several good books written about church reform in the wake of the pedophilia scandals. Among them are *The Coming Catholic Church: How the Faithful Are Shaping a New American Catholicism* by David Gibson (HarperSanFrancisco, 2003), *Our Fathers: The Secret Life of the Catholic Church in an Age of Scandal* by David France (Broadway Books, 2004), and *A People Adrift: The Crisis of the Roman Catholic Church in America* by Peter Steinfels (Simon & Schuster, 2003).

Readers interested in more contemporary feminist theology should take a look at *The Church and the Second Sex*, a classic work by Mary Daly (Beacon Press, 1985), or *In Memory of Her: A Feminist Theological Reconstruction of Christian Origins* by Elisabeth Schüssler Fiorenza (Crossroad/Herder, 1994). The first has a more political edge, the second is more theological. Also see *Beyond Patching: Faith and Feminism in the Catholic Church* by Sandra M. Schneiders (Paulist Press, revised, 2004).

This volume has already discussed one book by Gustavo Gutiérrez, the Peruvian founder of liberation theology. The classic work by Gutiérrez is *A Theology of Liberation* (Orbis Books, 1988). Also worth reading is *Introducing Liberation Theology* by Leonardo Boff and Clodovis Boff (Orbis Books, 1987).

We have not featured the giants of twentieth-century Catholic theology: Karl Rahner, Hans Urs von Balthasar, Bernard Lonergan, Edward Schillebeeckx. Several of their works were considered, but in the end they seemed just too technical for the average reader. Rahner and Lonergan are especially difficult, although Lonergan at least writes in English. Von Balthasar's *Love Alone Is Credible* received several recommendations to be included here (Ignatius Press, 2005). Schillebeeckx has three books worth exploring: *Christ: The Experience of Jesus as Lord* (Crossroad/Herder, 1983), *Church: The Human Story of God* (Crossroad/Herder, 1993), and *Christ: The Sacrament of the Encounter with God* (Sheed & Ward, 1995).

As for other works in theology, this volume already includes two works on Catholicism—by Karl Adam and Richard McBrien—but it only briefly mentions what may be the most famous of them all: Henri de Lubac's *Catholicism: Christ and the Common Destiny of Man* (Ignatius Press, 1988).

One of the crucial issues in theology in our day is the role of Christ in the salvation of the world. American Jesuit Roger Haight has made significant contributions to this topic through his books *Jesus, Symbol of God* (Orbis Books, 2000) and *The Future of Christology* (Continuum, 2005). The books have been praised by academic colleagues and attacked by the Vatican.

Saints' stories are as old as the church. Previously we mentioned *All Saints* by Robert Ellsberg. Another contemporary and good anthology is *Lives of the Saints: From Mary and Francis of Assisi to John XXIII and Mother Teresa* by Richard P. McBrien (HarperSanFrancisco, 2006). And of course you can still buy the twelve-volume set of *Butler's Lives of the Saints* from Liturgical Press, or the concise edition, revised and updated by Michael Walsh (HarperSanFrancisco, 1991). Elizabeth Johnson has written a fine theology of the saints in *Friends of God and Prophets* (Continuum, 1999). The canonization process is explained (and exposed) in Kenneth L. Woodward's book *Making Saints* (Touchstone, 1996).

There are always good single-volume biographies of the saints being published. Two of this author's favorites are *The Life of Thomas More* by Peter Ackroyd (Doubleday, 1998), and *Francis of Assisi: A Revolutionary Life* by Adrian House (HiddenSpring, 2001).

And if it's the popes, not the saints, you're interested in, then you should look at the two biographies by Peter Hebblethwaite, *Pope John XXIII* (Continuum, 2005) and *Paul VI: The First Modern Pope* (Paulist Press, 1993). *Witness to Hope* by George Weigel is considered the most authoritative life of Pope John Paul II (Harper Perennial, revised 2005).

Turning to general biography, for more of an insight on Flannery O'Connor see *The Habit of Being*, a collection of O'Connor's letters edited by Sally Fitzgerald (Farrar, Straus and Giroux, 1988). Frank McCourt's memoir of growing up in Ireland, *Angela's Ashes* (Scribner, 1999), certainly deserves mention. And the most comprehensive biography of Thomas Merton is *The Seven Mountains of Thomas Merton* by Michael Mott (Harvest Books/Harcourt, 1993).

Merton was going to be the only person represented in this volume by two titles, but in the end we took out *New Seeds of Contemplation* (New Directions, 1972); that book is still highly recommended. Of his other works we should particularly mention *The Sign of Jonas* (Harvest Books/Harcourt, 2002), a journal covering Merton's early years at Gethsemane. For those who would prefer an anthology of Merton writings, there is *Thomas Merton: Spiritual Master*, edited by Lawrence Cunningham (Paulist Press, 1992).

Spirituality makes up the largest single category in this book. One could go on and on recommending books of spirituality, including almost anything by Joyce Rupp, like her *Praying Our Goodbyes* (Ave Maria Press, 1988). The Paulist Press Classics of Western Spirituality have reawakened interest in mystical literature; several volumes in the series have been included here, but the series as a whole now amounts to nearly 120 volumes.

Because of space limitations there are just four more spirituality books that can be mentioned. One is the little book *Prayer* (Westminster John Knox Press, 1978) by Abhishiktananda, the Indian name of French Benedictine Henri Le Saux, but it is currently out of print. Second, Thomas Moore's *Care of the Soul*, so popular a decade ago, is still a sensitive and helpful book (Harper Perennial, 1994). This author had a small part in the publication of *Gratefulness: The Heart of Prayer* by David Steindl-Rast, and feels it deserves to be included in this list (Paulist Press, 1984). Finally, there is *Hope for the Flowers*, a classic fable with words and illustrations by Trina Paulus (Paulist Press, 1972). It's a book for all age groups and apparently for the ages, since its sales are approaching two million copies.

Turning to fiction, one wishes there were more Spanish or Latin American authors included in this volume. Few of the well-known contemporaries, however, have explored religious themes. And *Don Quixote*, although surely a great novel, didn't make the final cut because religious faith was not high on Cervantes's agenda.

Several fiction authors already represented in this volume have other works readers may want to explore. To begin with Flannery O'Connor, her *Wise Blood* (1952) and *The Violent Bear It Away* (1960), as well as her posthumous collection of stories *Everything That Rises Must Converge* (1965), are all published by Farrar, Straus and Giroux.

If you liked *The Moviegoer* you will like *The Second Coming* by Walker Percy (Picador, 1999). Mary Gordon's *Final Payments* (Anchor Books, 2006) could easily have stood alongside *Charming Billy* by Alice McDermott.

Some friends and colleagues who looked at this volume's list of one hundred titles felt that Graham Greene's *The Power and the Glory* (Penguin, 2003) should have been included, instead of *The End of the Affair.* The first is more explicitly Catholic, but they are both fine novels. See for yourself.

Other British novels that were left out include *Catholics*, by Brian Moore (Loyola Press, 2006), and the many novels by the late Muriel Spark. *The Girls of Slender Means* is considered her best work (New Directions, 1998).

Regarding novels published in recent years, *Atticus* by Ron Hansen (Harper Perennial, 1997) and *Empire Falls* by Richard Russo (Vintage, 2002) should be mentioned here.

And of course there are not just one hundred—or even a hundred and fifty—great Catholic books. There are thousands, and more are being published all the time. They are your friends and companions on the journey. Treasure them, hold them close. They tell you where you have come from, and where you are going.

BOOK NOTES

Abandonment to Divine Providence: Translated by and introduced by John Beevers, Jean-Pierre de Caussade's *Abandonment to Divine Providence* is available from Doubleday Image (1975). The book is also published as *The Sacrament of the Present Moment*, translated by Kitty Muggeridge and with an introduction by Richard J. Foster, by HarperSanFrancisco (1989).

After Virtue: Now in its third edition, *After Virtue* by Alasdair MacIntyre is available from University of Notre Dame Press (2007).

All Saints by Robert Ellsberg is published by Crossroad (1997).

An American Requiem by James Carroll is available from Mariner Books/Houghton Mifflin (1997).

Apologia pro Vita Sua: John Henry Newman's book was originally published with an introduction by Wilfrid Ward; the original edition can be found online at www .newmanreader.org.works.apologia/index.html. The Penguin edition (1994) is edited by Ian Kerr; the Norton edition (1968) is edited by David J. DeLaura; other editions are available from Kessinger Publishing (2004) and Dover Publications (2005).

Black Elk Speaks is available from Bison Books/University of Nebraska Press (2000). There is also an edition with added material by Alexis Petri and Lori Utecht from Bison Books (2004). The text can be found online at http://blackelkspeaks.unl.edu/.

Bread and Wine: Ignazio Silone's novel was reissued in 2005 by Signet/Penguin. *Bread and Wine* is one of a trilogy of novels by Ignazio Silone set in the village of Fontamara. The trilogy is available in English from Steerforth Italia (2000).

Brideshead Revisited by Evelyn Waugh is available in paperback from Little, Brown (1999) and in cloth from Everyman's Library (1993).

The Canterbury Tales: For readers who want a good, contemporary translation of Chaucer's tales, the Nevill Coghill translation is still considered the gold standard: Penguin Classics (1952, revised 2003). The Bantam edition (1982) is translated by A. Kent Hieatt and Constance Hieatt and has twenty-nine tales with Middle English on facing pages; the Oxford University Press edition (1998) has a translation by David Wright. The Middle

English original can be found at www.librarius.com/cantales. There are several online sites offering modern English versions; one can check them out at Google/Canterbury Tales.

A Canticle for Leibowitz: Walter Miller's novel is published by Bantam (1997).

Catholicism: The revised and updated third edition of Richard McBrien's *Catholicism* is available from HarperSanFrancisco (1994).

Charming Billy by Alice McDermott is published by Dell (1998).

Christian Zen by William Johnston is available from Fordham University Press (1997).

The Cloud of Unknowing: There are several good editions of this work. An edition translated by James Walsh is available from Paulist Press (1981). The Walsh text also appears in an edition with a foreword by Tim Farrington, HarperSanFrancisco (2004). William Johnston's translation, with an introduction by Huston Smith, is published by Doubleday Image (1996). A translation by Clifton Wolters is a Penguin Classics book (1978). Ira Progoff's translation is published by Dell (1957). An online version in Middle English can be found at www.lib.rochester.edu/camelot/teams/cloud.

Conferences: Nine of the twenty-four conferences are published as a paperback titled *John Cassian: Conferences*, translated by Colm Luibheid with an introduction by Owen Chadwick, in the Classics of Western Spirituality series, Paulist Press (1985). The complete text is available in cloth as *John Cassian: Conferences*, translated by Boniface Ramsey, in the Ancient Christian Writers series, Newman Press (1997). An online version translated by Edgar C. S. Gibson can be found at www.osb.org/lectio/cassian/conf/index.html.

The Confessions: There are several good editions of Augustine's *Confessions* in print, the most recent a translation by Garry Wills, Penguin Classics (2006). Also see the translation by Maria Boulding, Vintage (1998); the translation by Henry Chadwick, Oxford University Press (1991); the Doubleday Image edition (1960), translated by John K. Ryan; the edition translated in 1963 by Rex Warner, Penguin (2001). An online version can be found at http://ccat.sas.upenn.edu/jod/augustine.html.

Crossing the Threshold of Hope by Pope John Paul II is published by Knopf (1994).

The Dark Night: The classic by John of the Cross is available as *Dark Night of the Soul*, translated by Mirabai Starr, from Riverhead (2002), or, translated by E. Allison Peers, from Doubleday Image (1959). It is gathered with other writings in *The Collected Works of Saint John of the Cross*, translated by Kieran Kavanaugh and Otilio Rodriguez, ICS Publications (1991). A translation by William Whiston is available online at www.ccel.org/ccel/john_cross/dark_night.html.

Dead Man Walking: Helen Prejean's book is available from Vintage (1994).

The Dialogue: Especially recommended is the splendid translation by Suzanne Noffke published as *Catherine of Siena: The Dialogue*, in the Classics of Western Spirituality series,

Paulist Press (1980). A much older and abridged translation by Algar Thorold, *Dialogue of St. Catherine of Siena*, is available from Tan Books (1974). The Thorold translation can also be found online at http://www.cfpeople.org/books/dialog/cfptoc.htm.

The Diary of a Country Priest: As translated by Pamela Morris and introduced by Rémy Rougeau, Georges Bernanos's novel is available from Carroll & Graf (2002).

The Divine Comedy: John Ciardi's translation is probably the best known, although now more than fifty years old; it is published by New American Library (2003). Also see the Mark Musa translation in three volumes from Penguin Classics (2002), Allen Mandelbaum's translation with Italian on facing pages, Bantam (2004), and Robert Durling's translation in one volume from Oxford University Press (2007). Readers may also want to look into Robert Pinsky's *terza rima* translation of *The Inferno of Dante*, Farrar, Straus and Giroux (1994). English and Italian versions of the *Commedia* can be found at several online sites.

The Documents of Vatican II: There are two English translations of the council documents in wide use. The recommended version is *Vatican Council II: Constitutions, Decrees, Declarations*, edited by Austin Flannery, Costello Publishing (1996). Ask for the completely revised Flannery edition using inclusive language. The other edition is *The Documents of Vatican II*, edited by Walter M. Abbott, Guild Press (1966). The council texts are also online at www.rc.net/rcchurch/vatican2.

The Edge of Sadness: Edwin O'Connor's novel has been reissued by Loyola Press (2005) with a new introduction by Ron Hansen.

The End of the Affair by Graham Greene is available from Penguin (2004).

The End of the Modern World: First published in English in 1956, *The End of the Modern World* is now available with another essay by Romano Guardini titled "Power and Responsibility" and with a foreword by Richard John Neuhaus, ISI Books (1998).

Enthusiasm: Ronald Knox's work has been reissued by University of Notre Dame Press (1994).

The Geography of Faith: Originally published by Beacon Press, the Thirtieth Anniversary Edition of Berrigan's and Cole's *The Geography of Faith* is available from SkyLight Paths (2001).

A Good Man Is Hard to Find is available as a single volume from Harvest Books/Harcourt (1977), or as part of *Flannery O'Connor: The Complete Stories*, Farrar, Straus and Giroux (2000), or as a section of *Collected Works of Flannery O'Connor*, Library of America (1988).

The Great Mysteries: Andrew Greeley's book was originally published by Seabury Press. The revised edition is available from Sheed & Ward (2003).

A Guide for the Perplexed by E. F. Schumacher is available from Harper Perennial (1978).

Heart of Darkness by Joseph Conrad comes in many editions and formats. There is a hardback edition from Everyman's Library (1993), trade paperbacks from Hesperus Press (2003) and Penguin Classics (2000), and an inexpensive version from Dover Publications (1990).

The Holy Longing by Ronald Rolheiser is published by Doubleday Image (2007).

How the Irish Saved Civilization: Thomas Cahill's book is published as a handsomely illustrated paperback by Anchor Books (1996).

The Imitation of Christ: As mentioned, there are at least a dozen editions of Thomas à Kempis's *Imitation* for sale, but many of them are dated. Recommended are the translation by Joseph N. Tylenda, with a preface by Sally Cunneen, Vintage (1998), and the translation by William C. Creasy from Ave Maria Press (1989). Readers may also want to look at the "contemporary version" by William Griffin with a preface by Richard J. Foster, HarperCollins (2000). The text is available online as an unattributed "modern" translation at www.leaderu.com/cyber/books/imitation/imitation.html.

The Interior Castle: The translation by Kieran Kavanaugh and Otilio Rodriguez is rated the best by scholars. It appears in *The Collected Works of St. Teresa of Avila*, vol. 2, from ICS Publications (1980), as well as in *Teresa of Avila: The Interior Castle*, Classics of Western Spirituality, Paulist Press (1979), and in *Teresa of Avila: Selections from The Interior Castle*, edited by Emilie Griffin with a foreword by Patricia Hampl, HarperSanFrancisco (2004). There is also a recent translation of *The Interior Castle* by Mirabai Starr, Riverhead (2003). Doubleday Image (1972) uses an older translation by E. Allison Peers, which can also be found online at www.catholicfirst.com/thefaith/catholicclassics/stteresa/castle/interiorcastle.cfm, or at www.catholic-forum.com/Saints/stt01001.htm.

Introduction to the Devout Life: There is no contemporary, authoritative edition of Francis de Sales's *Introduction* to recommend. The late John K. Ryan was the translator of the best-known English version (1950), reissued by Doubleday Image (1972). A Vintage edition (2002) is handsome but based on an older translation. An "interpretation" of the *Introduction* is offered by Bernard Bangley, Shaw Books/Random House (2002); and the Cistercian monk William A. Meninger has an "adapted version" published as *The Committed Life*, Continuum (2001). Tan Books (1990) publishes an abridged version. An online edition is available at www.ccel.org/ccel/desales/devout_life.iv.html.

An Introduction to the New Testament by Raymond E. Brown is available from Anchor Books (1997).

Journal of a Soul: First published in the United States by McGraw-Hill, Pope John XXIII's *Journal of a Soul*, translated by Dorothy White, is now available from Doubleday Image (1999).

Kristin Lavransdatter: The Tiina Nunnally translation of Sigrid Undset's trilogy comes as three separate paperbacks, or as one large paperback, from Penguin (2005). The Charles Archer translation is sold as one hardback volume by Knopf (1985), or as three paperback volumes from Vintage (1987).

Lamy of Santa Fe: First published to much acclaim more than thirty years ago, Paul Horgan's biography of Archbishop Lamy has been reissued by Wesleyan University Press (2003). His *Great River*, the history of the Rio Grande, has also been reissued by Wesleyan (in two volumes), and his novel *Things As They Are* was recently reissued by Loyola Press.

The Letters of Abelard and Heloise, translated and with an introduction by Betty Radice, is available from Penguin (2004). Portions of letters and the *Historia calamitatum* can be found at several online sites.

The Liberation of the Laity by Paul Lakeland is available from Continuum (2004).

Life in a Jewish Family: Translated by Josephine Koeppel, Edith Stein's autobiography is available from ICS Publications (1986).

The Life of Antony: Writings by Athanasius fall into the category of patristics, published in multi-volume series with scholarly apparati. One such is *The Life of St. Antony*, edited and translated by Robert T. Meyer, Volume 10 in the Ancient Christian Writers series, Newman Press (1978). The most popular edition is *Athanasius: The Life of Antony and the Letter to Marcellinus*, translated and with an introduction by Robert C. Gregg, Classics of Western Spirituality, Paulist Press (1980). Also see the version contained in *Early Christian Lives*, translated and edited by Carolinne White, Penguin (1998), and *St. Antony of the Desert*, Tan Books (1995). The text is available online at www.ccel.org/fathers2/NPNF2-04/Npnf2-04-38.htm.

The Life You Save May Be Your Own by Paul Elie is available from Farrar, Straus and Giroux (2004).

The Little Flowers of St. Francis of Assisi: Doubleday Image (1958) has a version of the *Little Flowers* that was translated and edited by Raphael Brown more than fifty years ago. Vintage (1998) offers an adapted version of an even older translation by W. Heywood, spruced up with a new preface by Madeleine L'Engle. (The Heywood translation contains fewer stories than the Brown version.) And in 2006 New Seeds Books/Shambhala published a selection of stories newly translated by Robert H. Hopcke and Paul Schwartz. An online version of the *Little Flowers* can be found at www. franciscanfriarstor.com/stfrancis/Little_Flowers_St_Francis/index.htm.

The Long Loneliness by Dorothy Day was published in 1952 by Harper & Row (which later became HarperCollins). The 1997 edition has an introduction by Robert Coles.

The Lord of the Rings by J. R. R. Tolkien is published in the United States by Del Rey/Random House and by Houghton Mifflin. It is sold by Del Rey as three separate paperback volumes (1986, 1988, 1999), or as a paperback boxed set along with *The Hobbit* (2001). Houghton Mifflin editions include three boxed hardbacks (2003) or single paperback and hardback volumes (2005).

A Marginal Jew: John P. Meier's *A Marginal Jew* is both the title of his series and the title of the first volume in the series. The first three volumes are available from Doubleday (1991, 1994, 2001). At this writing the fourth and final volume was not yet available.

Mariette in Ecstasy by Ron Hansen is available from Harper Perennial (1991).

The Ministry of Reconciliation by Robert Schreiter is available from Orbis Books (1998).

Models of the Church: First published in 1974, Avery Dulles's *Models of the Church* is available from Doubleday Image (2002). The latest edition carries a new chapter on the ecclesiology of Pope John Paul II.

The Montessori Method can be purchased from Schocken Books (1964), or found online at www.digital.library.upenn.edu/women/montessori/method/method.html.

Morte D'Urban by J. F. Powers, with a new introduction by Elizabeth Hardwick, has been reissued as a New York Review of Books Classic (2000).

The Moviegoer: Walker Percy's novel is available from Vintage (1998).

Open Mind, Open Heart is published by Continuum both as a single volume (2006) and combined with other works by Thomas Keating in a volume titled *Foundations for Centering Prayer and the Christian Contemplative Life* (2002).

Orthodoxy: There are several editions of G. K. Chesterton's *Orthodoxy* in print. Paperbacks are available from Doubleday Image (1991), Ignatius Press (1995), and Continuum (2001). A cloth edition with a foreword by Philip Yancey was published by WaterBrook Press (2001). Another cloth edition is available from Hendrickson Publishers (2006). Finally, there's an annotated edition from Reformation Press (2002). The text is available online at www.cse.dmu.ac.uk/~mward/gkc/books/orthodoxy/index.html.

Parzival by Wolfram von Eschenbach, translated by A. T. Hatto, is available from Penguin (1980).

Pensées: Translated and revised by A. J. Krailsheimer, Blaise Pascal's *Pensées* is available from Penguin Classics (1995). A more recent translation by Roger Ariew is published by Hackett Publishing (2005). Also see the edition from Dover Publications (2003), translated by W. F. Trotter, with an introduction by T. S. Eliot. The Trotter translation is also available online at www.ccel.org/ccel/pascal/pensees.html.

The Phenomenon of Man: Teilhard de Chardin's work, translated by Bernard Wall and with an introduction by Julian Huxley, is available from HarperCollins. The translation was slightly revised in 1965.

Pilgrim at Tinker Creek: The twenty-fifth anniversary edition of *Pilgrim at Tinker Creek* wih a new afterword by Annie Dillard is available from Harper Perennial (1998).

Poems: Hopkins's poetry is available as *Gerard Manley Hopkins: A Selection of His Poems and Prose*, edited by W. H. Gardner, Penguin (1953), *Gerard Manley Hopkins: The Major Works*, edited by Catherine Phillips, Oxford University Press (2002), *Mortal Beauty, God's Grace: Major Poems and Spiritual Writings*, from Vintage (2003), and *God's Grandeur and Other Poems*, Dover Publications (1995).

The Practice of the Presence of God: There are numerous editions of *The Practice* by Brother Lawrence; a recommended translation is by Salvatore Sciurba, ICS Publications (1994). A recent edition with a foreword by Tessa Bielecki is published by New Seeds Books/Shambhala (2005). An online version can be found at www.PracticeGodsPresence.com.

Prayers and Meditations: In fact Anselm of Canterbury never wrote a book of prayers and meditations; rather, these were assembled long after his death. A book of that title, translated by Benedicta Ward, is available from Penguin (1973).

Primary Speech by Ann Belford Ulanov and Barry Ulanov is available from Westminster John Knox Press (1982).

Prison Writings: *Alfred Delp, SJ: Prison Writings*, with an introduction by Thomas Merton, Orbis Books (2004), is a recommended edition. Also see *With Bound Hands: A Jesuit in Nazi Germany: The Life and Prison Letters of Alfred Delp* by Mary Francis Coady, Loyola Press (2003).

The Reed of God: First published in 1944, *The Reed of God* by Caryll Houselander was recently reissued by Ave Maria Press (2006).

Religion and the Rise of Western Culture: Christopher Dawson's book was first published in the United States by Sheed & Ward. It is now available from Doubleday Image (1991).

Rerum Novarum can be found as an edition from Pauline Books and Media (2000), or as part of a larger volume titled *The Great Encyclical Letters of Pope Leo XIII (1878–1903)* from Tan Books (1995). The text is available online at www.papalencyclicals.net/Leo13.

Return to the Center is available from Templegate Press (1982), publishers in the United States of all books by Bede Griffiths.

Revelations of Divine Love: Julian of Norwich claimed to have had sixteen revelations that she described in twenty-five brief chapters (short text) or eighty-six chapters (long text). Most editions include both texts. There are numerous editions of Julian's work available. The best of them are probably *Julian of Norwich: Showings*, translated and with an introduction by Edmund Colledge and James Walsh, Paulist Press (1978); *The Showings of Julian of Norwich*, edited by Denise N. Baker, W. W. Norton (2004); and *Revelations of Divine Love*, translated by A. C. Spearing, Penguin (1999). Still other editions are published by Liguori, D. S. Brewer, Templegate, and Dover Publications. An online version in Middle English can be found at www.lib.rochester.edu/camelot/teams/julianfr.htm.

The Rule of St. Benedict: There are more editions of the rule in print than one can reasonably list. They include the Doubleday Image edition, translated in 1975 by Anthony C. Meisel and M. L. del Mastro, and the Vintage edition (1998), edited by Timothy Fry with a preface by Thomas More. Liturgical Press publishes several editions: a gift edition translated by Leonard J. Doyle published in 2001, a 1980 pamphlet version edited by Timothy Fry, and a 1996 edition translated and with a commentary by Terrence G. Kardong. Plus there is a translation with commentary by Joan Chittister, published as *The Rule of Benedict: Insights for the Ages*, Crossroad (1992). An online version translated by Boniface Verheyen can be found at www.osb.org/rb.

Sadhana: As is the case with nearly all of Anthony de Mello's titles, *Sadhana* is available from Doubleday Image (1984).

Saints and Sinners, by Eamon Duffy, first published in 1997 and revised in 2001, is available as a paperback from Yale University Press (2006).

Sayings and Stories: The sayings and stories of the Desert Fathers were assembled from the oral tradition and from other early Christian sources, so no two collections are alike. Still, the most complete English edition of desert stories, *The Sayings of the Desert Fathers*, edited by Benedicta Ward, organizes them according to author and is published by Cistercian Publications (revised 1987). *The Desert Fathers: Sayings of the Early Christian Monks* organizes them thematically and is published by Penguin Classics (revised 2003). A short collection of sayings illustrated by Yushi Nomura and with an introduction by Henri Nouwen was published as *Desert Wisdom*, Orbis Books (2000). Thomas Merton edited his own short collection of desert stories and gave it the title *The Wisdom of the Desert*, New Directions (1960). Many of the stories can be found online by going to Google/Desert Fathers.

Scivias: Hildegard's text appears in its entirety in the Classics of Western Spirituality volume *Hildegard of Bingen: Scivias*, translated by Mother Columba Hart and Jane Bishop, Paulist Press (1990). There is also an edition translated by Bruce Hozeski and titled

Hildegard of Bingen's Mystical Visions, Bear & Company (1985). Portions of *Scivias* are contained in *Selected Writings of Hildegard of Bingen*, translated by Mary Atherton, Penguin (2001), and in *Secrets of God: Writings of Hildegard of Bingen*, selected and translated by Sabina Flanagan, Shambhala (1996).

The Selected Poetry of Jessica Powers, edited by Regina Siegfried and Robert F. Morneau, was initially published by Sheed & Ward and reissued by ICS Publications (1999).

Selected Stories by Andre Dubus is published by Vintage (1996).

Sermons: Meister Eckhart never collected his sermons, so technically he never published a "book" of them. In fact some of his sermons were not recovered in manuscript form until the nineteenth century. Still, they appear today in two volumes of the Paulist Press Classics of Western Spirituality, *Meister Eckhart: The Essential Sermons, Commentaries, Treatises*, edited and translated by Bernard McGinn and Edmund Colledge (1981), and *Meister Eckhart: Teacher and Preacher*, edited and translated by Bernard McGinn and Frank Tobin (1987). Also available are *Treatises and Sermons of Meister Eckhart*, edited and translated by James M. Clark and John V. Skinner, Octagon Books (1983); *Meister Eckhart: Selected Writings*, edited and translated by Oliver Davies, Penguin (1994); and *Meister Eckhart: Selections from His Essential Writings*, HarperSanFrancisco (2005). Brief selections are available online at www.geocities.com/Athens/Acropolis/5164/eckhart.htm.

The Seven Storey Mountain by Thomas Merton is available from Harcourt, Brace with a 1998 introduction by Robert Giroux and a note to the reader by William H. Shannon.

She Who Is: First published in 1992, the Tenth Anniversary edition of this Elizabeth Johnson book was published by Crossroad in 2002.

A Short Account of the Destruction of the Indies: Las Casas's *Short Account*, as translated by Nigel Griffin, is available from Penguin (1992). It is also available under the title *The Devastation of the Indies: A Brief Account*, translated by Herma Briffault, from Johns Hopkins University Press (1992).

Silence by Shusaku Endo, translated and with a preface by William Johnston, is published by Taplinger (1980).

The Soul's Journey into God by Bonaventure, translated and introduced by Ewert Cousins, is available in the Classics of Western Spirituality series, Paulist Press (1978). Philotheus Boehner's translation, under the title *The Mind's Journey to God*, is available from Hackett Publishing (1993). Latin and English versions of *Itinerarium* can be found online at www.franciscan-archive.org/bonaventura/.

The Spirit of Catholicism: Karl Adam's book with an introduction by Robert A. Krieg is available from Crossroad/Herder (1997), and can be read online at www.ewtn.com/library/theology/spircath.htm.

The Spirit of Medieval Philosophy by Étienne Gilson is available from University of Notre Dame Press (1991).

Spiritual Exercises: Recommended editions include *Draw Me into Your Friendship: The Spiritual Exercises*, literal translation by Elder Mullan, with a contemporary reading by David L. Fleming, Institute of Jesuit Sources (1996); *The Spiritual Exercises of Saint Ignatius*, translated with a commentary by George A. Ganss, Loyola Press (1992); *Spiritual Exercises of Saint Ignatius*, translated by Louis J. Puhl, Vintage (2000); *Ignatius Loyola: Spiritual Exercises*, translated by Joseph A. Tetlow, Crossroad (1992). An online version can be found at www.jesuit.org/images/docs/915dWg.pdf.

Story of a Soul: The recommended edition is translated and edited by John Clarke, ICS Publications (1996). The Clarke translation also appears in *Thérèse of Lisieux: Essential Writings*, edited by Mary Frohlich, Orbis Books (2003).

The Tragic Sense of Life by Miguel de Unamuno, translated by J. E. Crawford Flitch, is available from Cosimo Classics (2005). A translation by Anthony Kerrigan is published by Princeton University Press (1978).

Utopia by Thomas More, translated by Clarence H. Miller, is available from Yale University Press (2001).

Vatican Council II: These collected articles by Xavier Rynne/Francis X. Murphy are published by Orbis Books (1999).

Vipers' Tangle: The François Mauriac novel, translated by Gerard Hopkins and with a new introduction by Robert Coles, has been reissued by Loyola Press (2005).

Virgin Time by Patricia Hampl is available from Farrar, Straus and Giroux (2005).

Waiting for God: Simone Weil's book originally appeared in French as *Attente de Dieu* (1950). When published in Britain it carried the title *Waiting on God*. However, the American publisher changed it to *Waiting for God*. Translated by Emma Crauford, it still carries that title, and is now published by Harper Perennial (2001).

We Drink from Our Own Wells: The twentieth anniversary edition of Gustavo Gutiérrez's *We Drink from Our Own Wells* is available from Orbis Books (2003).

We Hold These Truths: Originally published in 1960, this John Courtney Murray book is available from Sheed & Ward (2005).

Why I Am Still a Christian by Hans Küng is now available from Continuum (2005).

Word into Silence: First published in 1981 by Paulist Press, John Main's *Word into Silence* has been reissued by Continuum (1998).

The Wounded Healer by Henri Nouwen is available from Doubleday Image (1972).

INDEX

Abelard, Peter, 13–14
Aberdeen, university of, 77
Abhishiktananda, 204
Abraham, patriarch, 49
Ackroyd, Peter, 38, 203
Adam, Karl, 73–74, 202
Agnes, saint, 187
Albert the Great, 25
Albigensians, 98
Alcuin, 182
Alençon, 59
Alexander VI, pope, 190
Alexandria, 3
Ambrose, 6
Anselm of Canterbury, 7, 11–12
Antony, saint, 3–4
Apocalypse Now, 62
Archer, Charles, 72
Arians, 4, 12, 190
Aristotle, 19, 78, 92, 146, 152
Arlington, 184
Arthur, king, 17–18
Assisi, 21, 175–76
Athanasius, 3–4
Auden, W. H., 31, 106
Augustine of Hippo, 5–6, 101
Auschwitz, 162
Avignon, 29
Awareness: The Perils and Opportunities of Reality, 148

Barcelona, 39
Barnard College, 155
Barth, Karl, 12
Basil the Great, 10
Bec, monastery of, 11
Belgium, 37
Belloc, Hilaire, 145
Benedict of Nursia, 7, 9–10, 152
Benedict XVI, pope, 91, 124, 143
Benedicta of the Cross, see Edith Stein
Benedictine Priory of Montreal, 153
Benedictines, 9, 11, 37, 93, 141, 153
Bergamo, 122
Berlin, 109
Bernanos, Georges, 81–82
Bernard of Clairvaux, 14–15, 24, 157
Berrigan, Daniel, 129–30
Berrigan, Philip, 129
Bethlehem, 7
Bible, 9, 35, 73, 98, 108, 171–72, 174, 178, 185–87
Birmingham, England, 55

Black Death, 29, 34, 71
Black Elk, xv, 75–76
Black Elk's Religion, 75
Black Panthers, 130
Bloy, Léon, 99
Boff, Clodovis, 202
Boff, Leonardo, 198, 202
Bologna, 92
Bonaventure, 19–21, 24, 77
Boniface, saint, 182
Book of Hours, 11, 69
Borgia, family, 29
Boston, 128, 166, 183
Boston University, 183
Breslau, 162
Bridges, Robert, 70
Brown, Raymond E., xvi, 185–86
Buber, Martin, 180
Buddhism, 26, 131–32, 160, 179
Buffalo Bill's Wild West Show, 75
Burgos, 42
Butler, Alban, 187–88

Caen, 59
Cahill, Thomas, 92, 181–82
Calhoun, Rory, 115
Calvin, John, 45
Calvinism, 45
Cambridge University, 55, 90, 189
Camus, Albert, 180
Canada, 153, 195
Canterbury, 11, 31
Carmelites, 43, 47, 51, 59, 161, 167–68
Carolingian Empire, 92, 189
Carroll, James, 183–84
Carroll, Joseph, 183–84
Cassian, John, xiv, xv, 1, 7–8, 131, 153
Catechism of the Catholic Church, xvi, 143
Cather, Willa, 139
Catherine of Siena, 29–30
Catholic Theological Society of America, 114
Catholic Theological Union, 192
Catholic Worker, 102
Catonsville, 129
Caussade, Jean-Pierre de, 53–54
Cavett, Dick, 76
Celts, 181–82
Chambers, Whittaker, 101
Charlemagne, emperor, 182
Charles the Bald, emperor, 182
Chaucer, Geoffrey, 31–32

Chesterton, G. K., xv, 63–64, 145
Chiapas, 42
Chicago, 101, 128, 144, 184, 192
China, 103
Chrétien de Troyes, 17
Ciardi, John, 24
Cistercians, 28, 163, 176
Civiltà Cattolica, 124
Cloud of Unknowing, 33, 131
Cluny, abbey, 92
Cold War, 184
Coles, Robert, 129–30
Cologne, 25
Columbanus, saint, 182
Columbia University, 90, 155
Columbus, Christopher, 42
Congar, Yves, 180, 198
Conrad, Joseph, 61–62
Constantine, emperor, 1
Constantinople, 7
Contemplative Outreach, 164
Coppola, Francis Ford, 62
Counter-Reformation, 45
Cousins, Ewert, 20
Creative Ministry, 133
Cuba, 42
Cunningham, Lawrence, 204
Custer, George Armstrong, 75

Daly, Mary, 202
Daniélou, Jean, 198
Dante Alighieri, 23–24, 145
Darwin, Charles, 103
Dawson, Christopher, 91–92
Day, Dorothy, 63, 101-02, 188, 199–200
Death Comes for the Archbishop, 139
de Beaufort, abbé, 51–52
Declaration of Independence, 113
Decline and Fall of the Roman Empire, 181
De Gaulle, Charles, 82
Delp, Alfred, 109–10
de Lubac, Henri, 149, 180, 188, 198,
    202
De Mello, Anthony, 147–48
DeMello Spirituality Center, xvi
Denver, 140
de Sales, Francis, 45–46, 122
Desert Fathers, xiv, 1–2, 7–8
Devotio Moderna, 35
Dewey, John, 66
Dickinson, Emily, 168
Dillard, Annie, 137–38
Divino Afflante Spiritu, 185
Documents of Vatican II, xvi
Dominic, saint, 25, 95
Dominicans, 25, 92
Don Quixote, 68, 205
Donatists, 98
Dostoyevsky, Fyodor, 200
Dubus, Andre, 165–66
Duffy, Eamon, 189–90
Dulles, Avery, 135–36
Duns Scotus, 77
Durango, 140
Durling, Robert, 24

Ealing Abbey, 153
Ecclesiam Suam, 74
Eddy, Mary Baker, 98
Edict of Milan, 1
Edmonton, 196
Egeria, 1
Egypt, 1, 7, 103, 158
El Paso, 140
Elias of Crotona, 21
Elie, Paul, 199–200
Eliot, T. S., 17
Elizabeth of Hungary, saint, 187
Ellsberg, Robert, 187–88, 203
Endo, Shusaku, 125–26
England, 90, 106, 145
Episcopalians, 155
Erasmus, Desiderius, 78
Eriugena, John Scotus, 182
Ethics, of Spinoza, 161
Eugenius III, pope, 15
Eusebius, 172
Exodus, book of, 158

Fairfield University, 197
Farnsworth, Elizabeth, 194
Federal Bureau of Investigation, 183–84
Fénelon, François, 52, 98
Ferdinand II, king, 42
Fioretti, see Francis of Assisi
Fitzgerald, Sally, 203
Florence, 23, 29
Fordham University, 174
France, 50, 53, 59, 80–81, 90, 93, 103–04,
    139–40
France, David, 202
Francis of Assisi, 19, 21–22, 92, 101
Francis Xavier, 125
Franciscans, 19–22, 139, 175–76
Franco, Francisco, 82
Frankfurt, 162
Freiburg, university of, 162
French Revolution, 57
Frings, Josef, 128

Galileo, 188
Gandhi, Mohanhas, 188
Geneva, 45
George, saint, 187
Germany, 15, 73, 109, 145,
Gethsemane Abbey, 90, 168, 204
Gibbon, Edward, 181
Gibson, David, 201
Gill, Eric, 145
Gilson, Étienne, 77–78
Global Ethic Foundation, 160
Golden String, 141
Gordon, Carolyn, 199
Gordon, Mary, 205
Grail, 17–18
Greeley, Andrew M., 143–44
Greene, Graham, 89, 99–100, 205
Gregory XI, pope, 29
Griffiths, Bede, 141–42
Guardini, Romano, 95–96
Gutenberg, Johannes, xvi

Gutiérrez, Gustavo, 157–58, 202
Guzman, see Dominic

Haight, Roger, 203
Hampl, Patricia, 175–76
Hansen, Ron, 169–70, 205
Harter, Michael, 201
Harvard University, 77, 91, 129, 133
Harvey, Vernon and Elizabeth, 177–78
Hays, Edward, 201
Hebblethwaite, Peter, 203
Hegesippis, 172
Heidegger, Martin, 110
Heloise, 13–14
Henry VIII, king, 37–38
Herman, Nicholas, see Lawrence of the Resurrection
Hildegard of Bingen, 15–16
Hindus, 141, 153, 160
Hippo, city of, 5
Hispaniola, 42
Hitler, Adolf, 109
Holden, William, 115
Holler, Clyde, 75
Holocaust, 96
Hoover, J. Edgar, 183–84
Hopkins, Gerard Manley, 69
Horgan, Paul, 139–40
How the Irish Saved Civilization, 92
House, Adrian, 203
Houselander, Caryll, 85-86
Hugo Award, 112
Hundred Years War, 31, 34
Husserl, Edmund, 161

I Could Tell You Stories, 175
Ignatius Loyola, 12, 39–40, 45, 70, 148, 163
Ignatius of Antioch, 187
Illinois, university of, 101
India, 42, 66, 141, 148, 153, 174
Industrial Revolution, 57
Inquisition, 43
Introduction to the New Testament, xvi
Ireland, 132, 181–82, 193
Isaac, patriarch, 49
Islam, 160, 179
Italy, 66, 83, 112

Jackson, Peter, 105
Jacob, patriarch, 49
Jansen, Cornelius, 50
Jansenism, 46, 50, 98, 156
Japan, 125–26
Jerusalem, 39
Jesuits, 53, 70, 76, 103, 109–10, 113, 124, 125, 129, 131, 147, 203
Jews, 112, 160, 161–62, 179
John XXII, pope, 26
John XXIII, pope, 121–22, 124, 127–28, 184, 190
John, apostle, 11, 186
John Courtney Murray Award, 114
John of the Cross, 40, 47–48
John Paul I, pope, 35
John Paul II, pope, 26, 91, 143, 179–80, 187, 189–90, 203
John the Baptist, 11

Johns Hopkins University, 194
Johnson, Elizabeth A., 173–74, 203
Josephites, 129
Judaism, see Jews
Julian of Norwich, 33–34

Kant, Emmanuel, 73
Kasper, Walter, 173
Keating, Thomas, 154, 163–64
Kierkegaard, Søren, 115
King, Martin Luther Jr., 188
Kingsley, Charles, 55–56, 181
Knox, Ronald A., 85, 97–98
Koestler, Arthur, 101
Küng, Hans, 159–60, 198

Lakeland, Paul, 197–98
Lamy, Jean Baptist, 139–40
Las Casas, Bartolomé de, 41–42
Last Hurrah, 117
Latin America, 157–58, 191
Lawrence of the Resurrection, 51–52
Leo I, pope (the Great), 189
Leo X, pope, 190
Leo XIII, pope, 57–58
Lerner & Lowe, 17
Le Saux, Henri, see Abhishiktananda
Lewis, C. S., xiv, 31, 63–64, 141
Liberation theology, 150, 157, 202
Liénart, Achille, 128
Lisieux, 59
Little Big Horn, 75
Lives of the Fathers, Martyrs and Other Principal Saints, 187
Lombards, 10
London, 85, 87, 93, 99
Lonergan, Bernard, 202
Longfellow, Henry Wadsworth, 24
Lourdes, 175–76
Luther, Martin, 78

Machebeuf, Joseph, 139–40
MacIntyre, Alasdair, 151–52
Madrid, 68
Magyars, 92
Maimonides, Moses, 145
Main, John, 7, 153–54
Mainz, 95
Malory, Thomas, 17
Malraux, André, 180
Manchester, England, 98
Mandelbaum, Allen, 24
Manichaeans, 6
Manning, Henry, cardinal, 190
Marcion, 98
Marquette University, 168
Marseilles, 7
Martha, 8
Martin of Tours, saint, 187
Martin, Pauline, 59
Martin, Thérèse, see Thérèse of Lisieux
Martyrology, 187
Marxism, 151–52, 173
Mary Magdalene, 8
Mary, mother of Jesus, 11, 85–86, 149–50
Mary of Bethany, 8

Maurin, Peter, 102
Mauriac, François, 79–80
McBrien, Richard P., 149–50, 202–03
McCarthy, Mary, 200
McCourt, Frank, 203
McDermott, Alice, 193–94, 205
Medici, family, 29
Meier, John P., 171–72
Meister Eckhart, 25–26
Merton, Thomas, 77, 89–90, 101, 137, 168, 176, 196, 199–200, 204
Messori, Vittorio, 179
Methodists, 98
Mexican War, 139
Mexico, 42, 140
Millay, Edna St. Vincent, 168
Miller, Walter M., 111–12
Milton, John, 106
Minnesota, university of, 175
Miriam of the Holy Spirit, see Jessica Powers
Monica, 6
Monophysites, 190
Montanists, 98
Monte Cassino, 112
Montesinos, Antonio, 41
Montessori, Maria, 65–66
Montessori Society, 66
Monty Python, 17
Moore, Brian, 205
Moore, Thomas, 204
Moravians, 98
More, Thomas, 37–38
Morocco, 93
Moses, 27
Mott, Michael, 204
Munich, university of, 95
Murphy, Francis X., see Xavier Rynne
Murray, John Courtney, 113–14
Musa, Mark, 24
Mussolini, Benito, 66, 83–84
Mystical Body of Christ, 73, 136
Mystici Corporis, 74

Nancy, 53
National Book Award, 115, 120, 184, 194
National Socialism, see Nazis
Native Americans, 75–76
Nazis, 74, 80, 93, 109, 161, 190
Neihardt, John, xv, 7576
Netherlands, 35, 66, 161
New Orleans, 115–16, 199
New Testament, 171–72, 185–86
New York, city, 93, 101, 104, 168, 194
Newman, John Henry, 55–56, 70
Newman Theological College, 196
Nicaea, council of, 3–4
Nicene Creed, 143
Nobel Prize, 72, 80
Norsemen, 92
Norway, 71
Norwich, 33
Notre Dame University, 133, 149, 151, 157, 172
Nouwen, Henri, 133–34, 196
Nunnally, Tina, 72

Oblate School of Theology, 196
Oblates of Mary Immaculate, 196
O'Connor, Edwin, 117–18
O'Connor, Flannery, 107–08, 188, 199–200, 203, 205
Oriel College, 55
Orthodoxy, xv
Orwell, George, 88
Otto, Rudolf, 26
Our Man in Havana, 100
Oxford Movement, 70
Oxford University, 87, 98, 105, 141

Pachomius, 10
Paris, 13–14, 25, 51, 92, 122
Paris, university of, 182
Pascal, Blaise, 49–50
Patrick, saint, 181–82
Paul VI, pope, 74, 190
Paul, apostle, 8, 11, 136, 158, 172, 186
Paulus, Trina, 204
Peking Man, 103
Percy, Walker, 115–16, 199–200
Persia, 17
Peru, 42
Peter, apostle, 11, 189
Peter the Venerable, 14
Pine Ridge Reservation, 75
Pius IX, pope, 57, 190
Pius X, pope, 190
Pius XI, pope, 58, 190
Pius XII, pope, 74, 185, 190
Plato, 19, 78, 142
Poland, 161
Polo, Marco, 66
Pontifical Biblical Commission, 185
Pontifical Institute of Medieval Studies, 77
Portinari, Beatrice, 23
Powers, Jessica, 167–68
Powers, J. F., 119–20
Prejean, Helen, 177
Provincial Letters, 50
Pseudo-Dionysius, 24
Puerto Rico, 42
Pulitzer Prize, 118, 130, 137, 139–140, 177

Quadragisimo Anno, 58, 145
Quakers, 98
Quiet American, 100
Quietism, 53, 98

Rahner, Karl, 94–95, 202
Ratzinger, Joseph, 95; also see Benedict XVI
Reaching Out, 133
Reagan, Ronald, 130
Reformation, 45, 57
Rerum Novarum, 145
Ricoeur, Paul, 180
Rolheiser, Ronald, 195–96
Roman Empire, 91, 152, 181, 197
Romania, 7
Rome, 7, 10, 29–30, 57, 74, 83, 92, 121, 127–28, 181, 190
Rome, university of, 65
Roncalli, Angelo, see Pope John XXIII

Ronda, Bruce, 130
Rouault, Georges, 188
Rule of the Master, 10
Rupp, Joyce, 204
Russo, Richard, 205
Rynne, Xavier, 127–28

Salamanca University, 68
San Antonio, 196
San Francisco, 101
Santa Clara University, 169
Santa Fe, 139–140
Santo Domingo, 41
Sartre, Jean-Paul, 115
Sayers, Dorothy L., 24, 145
Scete, 1–2
Scharper, Philip, 113
Schillebeeckx, Edward, 198, 202
Schindler, Oskar, 188
Schneiders, Sandra M., 202
Scholasticism, 11, 35, 73, 78
Schreiter, Robert J., 191–92
Schumacher, E. F., 63, 145–46
Schüssler-Fiorenza, Elizabeth, 202
Scott, Sir Walter, 17
Seattle University, 196
Sebastian, saint, 187
Second Vatican Council, see Vatican Council II
Seville, 41, 68
Shakers, 98
Showings, see Julian of Norwich
Siena, 29
Silone, Ignazio, 83–84, 101
Sinai, 27
Sinclair, Upton, 101
Sioux, 75–76
Sisters of St. Joseph, 174
Small Is Beautiful, 145
Society of Jesus, see Jesuits
Song of Songs, 156
Sonnier, Patrick, 177–78
Sophia University, 131
Sorbonne, 77
Spain, 17–18, 41–42, 67–68, 82
Spanish Civil War, 82
Spark, Muriel, 205
Spender, Stephen, 101
Spinoza, Baruch, 161
Spirit of Catholicism, 149
Spiritual Exercises, 45, 70
Stein, Edith, 161–62
Steinfels, Peter, 202
Steindl-Rast, David, 204
St. John's College, 120
St. Joseph's Abbey, 163
St. Paul, city, 175
St. Peter's Basilica, 121
Strasbourg, 25
Summa Theologiae, xv
Suzuki, D. T., 26
Switzerland, 159
Syllabus of Errors, 57

Talmud, 145
Teilhard de Chardin, Pierre, 103–04

Teresa of Avila, 40, 43–45, 161
Thérèse of Lisieux, 35, 59–60, 175
Third Man, 100
Thirty Years War, 51
Thomas à Kempis, 35–36
Thomas Aquinas, xv, 19, 24–25, 77, 145
Thomas of Celano, 21
Tolkien, J. R. R., xvii, 105–06
Tolstoy, Leo, 101
Toronto, 77
Trent, council of, 190

Ugolino di Monte Santa Maria, 21
Ulanov, Ann Belford and Barry, 155–156
Unamuno, Miguel de, 67–68
Undset, Sigrid, 71–72
Union Theological Seminary, 155, 186
United States, 104, 139, 160, 178, 193
Urban, VIII, pope, 190

Vatican Council II, 73–74, 95, 113–14,
    117–18, 123–24, 127–28, 131, 133,
    135–36, 149, 180, 183, 185, 190,
    197–98, 200
Verba Seniorum, 1
Victoria, queen, 75
Vietnam War, 129, 183
Virgil, 23
Visigoths, 10
Visitation Sisters, 53
von Balthasar, Hans Urs, 202
von Hochheim, Eckhart, see Meister Eckhart

Wagner, Richard, 17
Wales, 18
Walsh, Michael, 203
Ward, Benedicta, 12
Waste Land, poem 17
Water Babies, 55
Waugh, Evelyn, 87–89, 98
Weathermen, 130
Weigel, George, 203
Weil, Simone, xv, 93–94
Weisskirchen, Austria, 162
Wesley, John, 35, 98
Westminster Abbey, 32
Wiesbaden, 184
Wilde, Oscar, 61
Willie, Robert Lee, 177–78
Wills, Garry, 5
Wittgenstein, Ludwig, 180
Wolfram von Eschenbach, 17–18
Woodward, Kenneth L., 203
World Community for Christian Meditation,
    153
World War I, 63, 106, 122, 162
World War II, 82–84, 86, 100, 105, 112, 117,
    120, 145, 193, 200
Wounded Knee, 75
Wright, Richard, 101

Yale University, 133
Ypres, 50

Zen, 2, 26, 131–32

ACKNOWLEDGMENTS

Scripture quotations are from the *New Revised Standard Version Bible*, copyright 1989 by the Division of Christian Education of the National Council of Churches of Christ in the United States of America. The quote about Abba Agatho in the Sayings and Stories of the Desert Fathers is from *The Wisdom of the Desert* translated by Thomas Merton (New Directions). The Garry Wills quote about the *Confessions* of Augustine is from his introduction to that volume (Penguin Classics). The comment by Barbara Newman about Hildegard of Bingen as a theologian is from her introduction to the Classics of Western Spirituality edition of *Scivias* (Paulist Press). Ewert Cousins's comment about Bonaventure's *Journey* is from his introduction to the Classics of Western Spirituality edition of *The Soul's Journey into God* (Paulist Press). The quotes by C. S. Lewis and W. H. Auden regarding Chaucer are from an article "Chaucer and Religion" by Brother Anthony of Taizé at www.luminarium.org/medlit/chaucer.htm. Peter Ackroyd's comments about *Utopia* appear in his biography of Thomas More (Doubleday). The remark of Pope Pius IX (mentioned in the entry *Rerum Novarum*) that slaves be true to their masters appears in his encyclical *Nostris Nobiscum* (1849), no. 33. The oft-quoted anecdote of G. K. Chesterton being "out at the front" can be found in A. N. Wilson's *Hilaire Belloc* (Penguin). Hopkins's letter to John Henry Newman appears in *Gerard Manley Hopkins: A Selection of His Poems and Prose* edited by W. H. Gardiner (Penguin). Thomas Merton's recollection of reading Étienne Gilson can be found in *The Seven Storey Mountain* (Harcourt, Brace). Tolkien's belief, expressed in a letter, that *The Lord of the Rings* is "fundamentally religious" has been quoted many times, for instance in "J. R. R. Tolkien: Truth and Myth" by Joseph Pearce, at catholiceducation.org/articles/arts/al0107.html. W. H. Auden's comments on Tolkien are from a review in the *New York Times*. Walker Percy was interviewed by John Griffin Jones in *Conversations with Walker Percy*, edited by Lewis A. Lawson and Victor A. Kramer (University Press of Mississippi). The comment by Benedict XVI regarding the teachings of the Second Vatican Council was carried by the Catholic News Service in February 2006. The original quote about "Mother Church" knowing best (mentioned in the entry *The Great Mysteries*) can be found at www.diocese-kcsj.org/flashLanding.html. De Mello's story of the fictional Master and his disciple appears in *More One Minute Nonsense* by Anthony de Mello (Loyola Press). Cardinal Kasper's remark about the "heresy of theism" can be found in Elizabeth A. Johnson's *She Who Is* (Crossroad). Thomas Cahill quotes Charles Kingsley in *How the Irish Saved Civilization* (Anchor Books). Alice McDermott's interview with Elizabeth Farnsworth was broadcast on PBS on November 20, 1998, and can be found at www.pbs.org/newshour/bb/entertainment/july-dec98/mcdermott_11-20.html.